Architecture and Leadership

From cathedrals to cubicles, people go to great lengths and expense to design their living and working environments. They want their spaces to be places where they enjoy being, reflecting who they are and what they care about. The resultant environments in turn become loud, albeit unvocal, leaders for people occupying those corresponding spaces. The design and use of work and living spaces typifies and thematizes expectations for the group. Essentially, the architecture of rooms, buildings, and cities creates cultures by conveying explicit and implicit messages. This is evident when people approach and walk into St. Basil's Cathedral in Moscow, the Forbidden City in Beijing, the Sydney Opera House in Sydney, Australia, the Jewish Museum in Berlin, or the Rothko Chapel in Houston, to name some examples.

While leaders oftentimes lack the resources to have their spaces mirror the greatest architectural achievements of the world, they are in a position to use the art and science of architecture, at whatever scale is available, to their advantage. The creative and intentional use of space and place advances and promotes cherished values and enhances organizational effectiveness. This book explores the essence of good architecture and establishes relevant connections for leaders and managers to strategically design and use the organizational workplace and space to support their mission and purpose, and create esthetically meaningful work environments. It equips leaders to be culturally astute on what defines good architecture and to incorporate principles of beauty in their leadership practices accordingly and will be of interest to researchers, academics, professionals, and students in the fields of leadership, organizational studies, and architecture theory and practice.

Mark A. Roberson is the Founding Dean of the College of Architecture, Visual Arts & Design at California Baptist University, USA.

Alicia Crumpton is an operations and leadership consultant, researcher, and writer.

Leadership Horizons

Series Editors

John Shoup, California Baptist University, USA

Troy Hinrichs, California Baptist University, USA

The original and timeless research on leadership is situated in the classical works associated with the humanities. Great literature, art, theatre, philosophy, and music provide both existential and visceral insights to the drama of leadership beyond what traditional approaches to leadership studies have been able to furnish up to now. The classics in the humanities are didactic commentaries on universal themes associated with the challenges and hopes of good leadership. Knowledge of the classics provides a way of appreciating historical and contemporary cultures and a framework for thinking deeply about what is true, good, honorable, and beautiful. Returning the classics to the leadership genre equips leaders with a culturally informed language and narrative to develop the often ignored aesthetical aspects of leadership. This series connects lessons from various great works in art, literature, philosophy, theatre, and music to specific leadership research and contemporary leadership challenges. The series weaves the art and science of leadership studies and equip readers with multiple frames of reference to become aesthetically pleasing, engaging, and culturally astute leaders to make the right things happen the right way.

Leadership Horizons is relevant to students and researchers across business and management, organizational and institutional studies, and the humanities.

Books in the series:

History and Leadership
The Nature and Role of the Past in Navigating the Future
Mark E. Blincoe and John R. Shoup

Architecture and Leadership
The Nature and Role of Space and Place in Organizational Culture
Mark A. Roberson and Alicia D. Crumpton

For more information about this series, please visit: www.routledge.com/ Leadership-Horizons/book-series/LH

Architecture and Leadership

The Nature and Role of Space and Place in Organizational Culture

Mark A. Roberson and Alicia D. Crumpton

NEW YORK AND LONDON

First published 2023
by Routledge
605 Third Avenue, New York, NY 10158

and by Routledge
4 Park Square, Milton Park, Abingdon, Oxon, OX14 4RN

Routledge is an imprint of the Taylor & Francis Group, an informa business

Library of Congress Cataloging-in-Publication Data
Names: Roberson, Mark, author. | Crumpton, Alicia D., author.
Title: Architecture and leadership : the nature and role of space and place
    in organizational culture / Mark Roberson and Alicia D. Crumpton.
Description: New York, NY : Routledge, 2023. | Includes bibliographical
    references and index.
Identifiers: LCCN 2022042659 | ISBN 9780367763619 (hardback) |
    ISBN 9780367764005 (paperback) | ISBN 9781003166788 (ebook)
Subjects: LCSH: Architecture—Human factors. | Organizational behavior. |
    Leadership.
Classification: LCC NA2542.4 .R59 2023 | DDC 720.1/03—dc23/
    eng/20220916
LC record available at https://lccn.loc.gov/2022042659

ISBN: 978-0-367-76361-9 (hbk)
ISBN: 978-0-367-76400-5 (pbk)
ISBN: 978-1-003-16678-8 (ebk)

DOI: 10.4324/9781003166788

Typeset in Times New Roman
by Apex CoVantage, LLC

Contents

Tables

Figures

Acknowledgments

Saying yes to writing a book on a topic that we are as passionate about as architecture and leadership seemed like the right thing to do in the moment. That neither of us had ever written a book seemed to pale in comparison to our shared enthusiasm for the topic. Perhaps we would have responded differently if we really considered the opportunities and challenges associated with conceiving of and writing a book. But for whatever reason, when John Shoup (Executive Director of the Dr. Paul and Annie Kienel Leadership Institute at California Baptist University) asked us to contribute an entry into the Routledge Focus on Interdisciplinary Perspectives on Leadership, we said yes. Thank you, John, for your belief in us and your generous mentoring and encouragement.

I, Mark, want to thank my wife Leslie, first and foremost. She is not only my most fervent supporter but also my sounding board for ideas and my first editor for everything I have written since I entered academia, including this book. And her chef-level cooking keeps me fueled for whatever task is at hand. And, to all of those who gave me advice and guidance along the way, many thanks to all of you.

I, Alicia, want to express my profound thankfulness for my husband Jonny who believes in my capacity to do anything I set my mind to. His belief propels me forward when I do not know what to write and start to think that the blankness of a page is all I know or have to say.

We also acknowledge and are grateful for our publishers Routledge, Taylor and Francis Group, and their editorial staff, Naomi Round Cahalin, Brianna Ascher, and Jessica Rech. Their approval of our book idea, combined with their support of two previously unpublished authors, was important to our belief that the concepts discussed herein needed a voice and a means by which to be communicated. Also, we want to state how appreciative we are for their scheduling flexibility and graciousness, as our best-laid plans were affected by the vagaries of life.

Special thanks to Rick Archer, Nathan Kim, and Jim McKinney for providing connections to some wonderful case study interviewees that we would have never been able to connect with otherwise. Finally, we acknowledge those we interviewed during our research and the scholars and practitioners who care about architecture and leadership. Their practical experience, scholarship, voices, and views about how the built environment and our lived experiences within it shapes identity and provide meaning and purpose are catalysts for optimism and hope.

Preface

Welcome to this entry into the Routledge Focus on Interdisciplinary Perspectives on Leadership. This series examines leadership through a unique lens provided by an understanding of the humanities. Whether you have previously read volumes on leadership and literature, leadership and philosophy, leadership and history, or if this is your first foray into this line of thinking, you have chosen what we believe will be an enlightening and applicable subject, serving you well in your pursuit of improved leadership. This book explores the specific subject of architecture and its connections to leadership, including applicable lessons for leaders.

Effective leaders are good designers. Organizational mission, vision, and strategies translate into organizational policies, structure, workflow, and communications to support a vision and sense of overall direction. These and other elements are taught in business, leadership, and organizational psychology classes as vitally essential elements to intentionally consider. However, the importance, impact, and potential of leveraging the physical environment is rarely taught, even though associated costs and potential effects related to our physical spaces greatly influence organizational success and human flourishing. The built environment influences the lived experiences of humans individually and collectively, affecting their work and capacity to meet organizational mission and goals.

Good leadership is based on the context of an organization's situation and is influenced by factors such as physical location, history, culture, politics, market drivers, customer demands, etc. Good architecture is also a resultant product emerging from all its influencing context. Good leaders tell good stories about their purpose, the organization, the people they're leading, and the people they want to reach. Good architecture also similarly tells stories about those who build, inhabit, and experience the physical environment. Good leaders also must take a long view of success and build a foundation that will last beyond themselves. Organizations are judged by their ability to succeed, remain effective over time, and adjust as necessary. Good architecture also stands the test of time and is considered worthy beyond any passing fad or initial stylistic statement. In all these ways (and more), good leadership and good architecture are related. They are also related in the outsized impact architecture has on the organization.

A major impetus for writing this book is to consider connections between architecture and leadership, connections that you can leverage intentionally to strategically influence your organizational identity, culture, climate, and structure.

Interdisciplinary Approach

This exploration specifically and intentionally used an interdisciplinary approach. One author is an architect, an academic, and is the dean of a college of architecture and design. In contrast, the other author holds a PhD in leadership studies and is a management consultant. Different academic backgrounds, career experiences, differing locations, one male, one female – all these factors contribute to an interdisciplinary exploration of the intersection of architecture and leadership. We spent over a year reading, drawing concepts on a whiteboard, and conversing about what we see and mean when we assert a connection between architecture and leadership. A by-product of our process is a recognition of what social psychologist Farrell (2001) called a collaborative circle where peers "through long periods of dialogue and collaboration, negotiate a common vision . . . including what constitutes good work, how to work, what subjects are worth working on, and how to think about them." Conversing about and synthesizing across disciplines further enhances our capacity to make connections between two fields of study: architecture and leadership studies. We hope that by better understanding architecture and its contributions to leadership, we might see ways to restore our human home and provide human flourishing, healing, and community.

How This Book is Organized

This book contains seven chapters. Chapter 1 explains what architecture actually is and why the built environment all around us matters so much. This includes how architecture affects and influences the social fabric of our lives and how this connects to the idea of leadership. Chapter 2 builds on the idea that there is a difference between the spaces we pass through and function within and the places that we inhabit in a more meaningful and life-affirming way. We propose that making places matters to us and to our organizations in the way these places contribute to identity, meaning, and purpose. The architecture that leaders provide is integral to their organizations inhabiting such meaningful places. In Chapter 3, we explore principles associated with the idea that architecture can be solidly assessed as good or bad. We describe these principles in terms of time, firmness, utility, and delight and propose potential effects of good architecture. Critical Components of Architecture, including Building Elements and Design Principles, are introduced and explored in Chapter 4. Chapter 5 describes specific Design Principles and their applications. Within Chapter 6, organizational context, culture, climate, and structure are explored in relation to leadership and architecture. Human and architectural values are defined as they represent the espoused and enacted values of leadership. These values are further translated into Use Strategies, including features to consider when designing a new space. Five case studies are explored in Chapter 7, representing various facets of the intersection of architecture and leadership, followed by a discussion of lessons learned.

How This Book Can Be Used

This book is designed for a nonacademic reader, specifically a leader interested in exploring the intersections of architecture and leadership. It is written in a more relaxed tone and approach to create accessibility and ease of use. Each chapter retains the unique voice of its primary author to deliberately highlight the differing ways people from discrete disciplines talk about this topic. This book about architecture and leadership melds the authors' mutual understanding into a single thread of thought.

Reference

Farrell, M. P. (2001). *Collaborative circles: Friendship dynamics & creative work.* University of Chicago Press.

1 Architecture and Leadership Connections

Introduction

Some years ago, I (Mark) went to a friend's church to pick her up on a Sunday night. She was there for choir practice, but I knew it was part of her church's DNA to hold worship services every Sunday night. As I approached their brand-new church building, I noticed that the parking lot was virtually empty. When my friend got in the car, I asked why so few people were there, and she explained that it cost too much to air condition the main auditorium for the number of people who typically attended on Sunday nights, and there wasn't another room in the new building suitable for holding Sunday night services. So as a result, the church decided to stop meeting on Sunday nights during the summer heat. I was astounded that only a few weeks into its occupation, this brand-new building, which cost so much time, money, effort, and emotion to build, was now determining how the church performed operationally.

There was great expectation and hope that this new building would help the church make strong connections to the young families filling this new growing neighborhood and that the ministry of the church would grow to meet the needs of this new community. Very quickly, however, the church's ministry efforts had to shrink to accommodate the building's limitations. It was surprising that a new, purpose-built structure would fall short of meeting the goals and functional needs of the church. The new building had all the physical elements of a church: a steeple, big stained-glass window, large auditorium, choir loft, nursery rooms, and even a gymnasium. When people in the neighborhood drove by and saw this building being constructed, they understood what the building would be and could infer its intended purposes. There was even some effort to make the building esthetically pleasing. However, it seemed that the design reflected some generic idea of what a *church* should look like, as opposed to uniquely responding to its specific purpose, neighborhood, and context. Something was lacking between the ideas that

DOI: 10.4324/9781003166788-1

shaped the design of the church and the translation of organizational vision, strategies, goals, and needed functionality into the finished design.

The purpose of this chapter is to describe the relationship between architecture and leadership to help leaders think differently about these challenges, and as an effort to help leaders build a more substantial social fabric for their organizations. Architecture's influence is described with an emphasis on how vital design intentionality is concerning organizational vision, mission, purpose, and goals, and how that critically contributes to the lived experiences of people, including their overall wellbeing.

Unfortunately, this church story is too often the norm with regard to design and this fact is not restricted to churches. Reflecting on your own past experiences of entering a new office, library, or museum, you might recall a sense that something was not quite right. For some reason, the building simply did not quite work the way it was supposed to, didn't connect to its intended audience the way it was hoped, or didn't engender organizational culture as envisioned. This narrative leads to questions about how – or if – leaders think about their architecture as a factor of success. Reflectively consider the following:

- Recall an experience where you thought positively or negatively about an architectural space.
- What specifically influenced your recalled experiences of architecture?
- Consider your organization, and specifically reflect on how your physical space influences or affects such things as organizational structure, information flow, workflow, collaboration, communication, and decision making.
- What esthetics affect your experience of a space? Consider things like color scheme, textures, sound, smell, curved or straight lines, amount of light, ability to see nature, etc.

Look around where you are currently sitting while reading this book and observe the environment. Those physical surroundings represent what we call the built environment, and all the ones you experience every day unconsciously affect you cognitively and emotionally, even when you aren't paying attention. To intentionally think about your life as surrounded by architecture might be a new and surprising thing to consider. The ways that architecture and leadership are integrally connected might also be something you haven't considered before. However, the power and influence of our built environment has, in fact, been intentionally considered and employed by those as disparate as the God of the Bible and the leader of Nazi Germany.

David, king of ancient Israel and the author of many of the Old Testament Psalms, spoke of how God used the physical environment He designed for the purposes of leading His people and the communication of His message in the Biblical poetry of Psalms 19:

> For the choir director: A psalm of David.
> 1 The heavens proclaim the glory of God.
> The skies display his craftsmanship.
> 2 Day after day they continue to speak;
> night after night they make him known.
> 3 They speak without a sound or word;
> their voice is never heard.
> 4 Yet their message has gone throughout the earth,
> and their words to all the world.
> (Psalm 19, New Living Translation)

Nazi architect Albert Speer's words for how Adolf Hitler intended the physical environments he created to affect and lead the people of Germany reveal the power of this topic as well:

> When Hitler spoke of the effect of a building he had planned, he always referred to its power of suggestion. He would talk enthusiastically about the farmer who would travel all the way from the provinces to Berlin, enter the Great Hall . . . [and feel] literally crushed by what he saw.
> (as cited in Lane, 2016)

These words of God's servant David and those of Hitler's favored architect Speer seem to implicitly draw our attention toward the enormous potential effects of our physical environment on human feeling and action, from the most sacred to the most profane.

Significance of the Topic

The purpose of this book is to equip leaders to observe the built environment with a deeper understanding, to gain an appreciation for how architecture and leadership are connected, and to consider why these connections matter to their organization. We believe this is a critical historical moment for many reasons to discuss the relationship between leadership and the humanities, particularly architecture. Leadership books, blogs, podcasts, and seminars are proliferating like never before, yet our societal direction seems to indicate that our leadership in practice is suffering more than ever. Indicators that our social fabric is unraveling are evidenced by declining societal and environmental health and effects related to a variety of causes, such as the ubiquitous use and adoption of technology, as well as numerous other segments of society that are in or are contributing to decline. Poet John O'Donohue (2000) expressed the challenge poignantly:

> Our world is facing so many crises ecologically, economically, and spiritually. These cannot be overcome by isolated individuals. We need to come together. There is incredible power in a community of people who are together because they care, and who are motivated by the ideals of compassion and creativity.

The ubiquity of the church's story described in the introduction illustrates that organizational leadership may be unwittingly pushing us into further decline despite best intentions. We hope to provide an opportunity as yearned for by O'Donohue to come together around a better understanding of ideas regarding the vital aspect of our built environment. This section discusses social fabric, perceptions of leadership, and our relationship to architecture.

This social fabric to which we refer is a metaphor representing the collective in terms of social order, processes, and norms (Short, 1984). Social fabric speaks to agency and action (weaving), the individual (a weaver but also part of the social fabric), and the collective (social fabric), which implies a shared history, connectedness, and context. Think of social fabric as our mutually agreed upon ways of living and being together. The weaving aspect of the phrase highlights that our experience of social fabric is constructed relationally and, perhaps, intentionally. Researcher Juliette Mackin (1997), in her exploration of the urban communities' social fabric, defined social fabric as "what holds societies together, maintains social order and sustains institutional forms" (p. 1).

Our built environment contributes to the social fabric by defining spaces within which people exist. Imagine a soccer field – there's the game and stands of people supporting their players and team. If we say the term *soccer moms*, you expand your understanding of soccer to include a suite of behaviors, actions, and ways of interacting with and supporting the team. In this sense, social fabric represents the entirety of what we think of when we think of soccer – where people gather in a place, share life together, and mutually agree to social norms or ways of behaving that are viewed as acceptable within the context. Architecture then shapes the social fabric in meaningful ways.

Architecture that we create and experience continues to lead and shape, reflecting society and the social fabric it serves. The subjects of architecture and leadership offer an opportunity for renewed consideration due to the interaction between architecture and a person's physical, mental, emotional, and spiritual health. The built environment refers broadly to "human-made physical spaces where we live, recreate and work. These include our buildings, furnishings, open and public spaces, roads, utilities and other infrastructure" (Collaborative, n.d.). Furthermore, the Collaborative on Health and Environment website (n.d.) identifies indoor, outdoor, and recreational environmental ill effects on our health, mental health, and socioeconomic status associated with the built environment.

Theologian Timothy Gorringe (2002) asserted that the built environment "provides us with all the most direct, frequent, and unavoidable images of everyday life, and is never just happenstance." As such, our built environment, including those places designated as work, interacts with our heart and being in tangible and intangible ways. Eco-architect Christopher Day (2014), in thinking about a psychology of architecture, noted:

> Art transcends the limitations of matter. It imbues the physical with spirit. To be surrounded by spirit-impregnated matter has a very different effect on us than being surrounded by dead matter. One sensitized us and motivates consciousness: the other deadens sensitivities and saps individuated will.
>
> (p. 4)

We see this as a call to understand, appreciate, and embrace the interactive and co-creative relationships between architecture and leadership – the bedrock, fundamental principles that sustain thriving, healthy human interaction, and a continued weaving of the social fabric. That these principles are made clear through a study of the principles of great architecture is not surprising, as we shall see. We aim to provide hope, a better path, and to provide concrete, applicable principles for all leaders to be able to do what they do better.

One of the things we know and can examine about leadership is that perspectives on leadership and the resulting theories that have presided over the subject have evolved over time. Chronologically thinking about leadership, organizations, and systems, we observe shifts in thinking from leader as individual, to leader as evaluator and influencer of follower and situation, to leader and follower in relationship and context. It is this latter thinking about collaborative and relational leadership relative to context, particularly physical context, that we seek to understand and advance. Architecture is influential, wielding a great deal of presence, power, and meaning in our lives and leadership.

Architecture's Influence

Designed and created artifacts encountered in daily life have an outsized influence on us. Architecture, media, art, photography, music, graphics, clothing, and films all shape our understanding of the world in which we live and our place in it. However, none of these have the same ability to affect us in so many tangible and intangible ways as the architecture in which we live, work, learn, worship, and play.

Eighteenth-century German philosopher Immanuel Kant (2003) posited that we understand the world by reflecting on our various experiences of it, and there are few things we experience so regularly as architecture. Architecture is a word used in many ways and referential to many contexts in contemporary culture. In part, architecture refers to just about anything that is *built*, including computer software, political systems, social movements, and more. However, the word has a precise meaning that is important for us to understand. In everyday language, architecture is described as "the art or practice of designing and building structures and especially habitable ones" (Merriam-Webster, n.d.). First, that the word architecture is defined as the designing and building of structures, is an important distinction that needs to be made from not only all other creative activities but also all other current uses of the word. Second, the word habitable is a crucial piece of that definition, in that architecture is not limited to the designing and building of external structures and facades that we see and recognize. It is not even simply the surfaces that bound rooms, that is, the walls, floors, and ceilings.

Most importantly, architecture is the space that is then defined by those surfaces that we inhabit, both interior and exterior. Walls, floors, and ceilings define the interior spaces of rooms, and exterior building facades define the exterior spaces of yards, courtyards, streets, piazzas, squares, and cities. Therefore, architects don't create space; they define space. Space already exists in the world, but the structures we compose and impose on the world define how we experience that space. It is then the definition of these spaces – their size, shape, proportion, circulation paths, materiality, relative transparency, color, and light – that determines their quality and effectiveness.

Walking into a building like St. Peter's Basilica in Rome (Figure 1.1), the rotunda in the U.S. Capitol building in Washington D.C. (Figure 4.20), or the Guggenheim Museum in New York City (Figure 5.10) can overcome a person with awe and wonder simply by the experience of the space just entered.

On the other hand, one might experience physical revulsion upon entering a shabby motel room; a run-down restaurant; or a dark, depressing office space. Perhaps you have experienced these reactions. If so, whether you realize it or not, you are mentally, emotionally, and even physically affected and influenced by the built environment. The built environment is not value-free or benign in its effect. We are constantly experiencing and

Figure 1.1 The grand interior space of St. Peter's Basilica, Vatican City, Italy. Photo
     by Mark A. Roberson.

responsively interacting with the built environment. This interplay of experience and response happens to everybody, all the time, and people have
well chronicled and commonly experienced visceral reactions to spaces and
places they inhabit and experience, even spaces and places that exist in

reference to things as disparate as the Heavens or Nazi Germany, as previously referenced.

In a 1943 speech to the House of Commons referencing the rebuilding plans for the House of Lords, which was bombed in WWII, then Prime Minister Winston Churchill summarized the eternal significance of that building project by declaring, "We shape our buildings and afterwards they shape us." He is referring to the influence of architecture. It is true that some buildings are considered beautiful and important, some evoke awe-inspired emotional reactions, some are endearing and enduring, and some evoke connection and attachment. It is through better understanding architecture in general that we can ascertain the causes and effects of the built environment that surrounds us every day; therein, improving the ability of our future built environments to integrally shape and support our organizations.

Interestingly, despite architecture's ever-present power and influence, and our collective recognition of its significance, the very world of architecture around us often goes unnoticed, not only because of its ubiquity but also because that ubiquity consists of more than these stately buildings that demand and deserve our attention. Yale School of Architecture professor Kurt W. Forster (1999) said, "architecture is so omnipresent in our lives that buildings have become our 'second nature' – so much so that, affecting us unconsciously, they seem frequently to obscure both nature and our own predicament." Humans are neurologically wired to ignore things around us that are constant, safe, and ubiquitous, yet those things still play a role in our mental processing. Architecture critic and writer Sarah Williams Goldhagen (2020) noted:

> Even when we pay no conscious attention to the built environment or focus only on selected aspects of it – that's nearly all the time – it functions, in our lived experience, as a never-ending concatenation of what some social psychologists call primes. A prime is a nonconsciously perceived environmental stimulus that can influence a person's subsequent thoughts, feelings and responses by activating memories, emotions and other kinds of cognitive associations.

Goldhagen (2020) goes on to say that "Our built environment is riddled with primes, and because it is, a design can be deliberately composed to nudge people to choose one action over another" (pp. 59, 61). Much of the architecture surrounding our everyday lives exists in this realm of second nature, and very much in the background. Unfortunately, some of it is in the background because it was never intended to be very noticeable or inspiring. But intended or not, the constructed second nature, as Forster (1999) and

Goldhagen (2020) pointed out, affects us as well. So, architecture surrounding us is good and bad, inspiring and insipid, overwhelming and unnoticed. It is many things all at once, but always present and affecting.

Chapter Summary

Architecture influences us mentally, emotionally, physically, and spiritually. People feel these effects all the time subconsciously, as we spend our lives within architecture. The built environment dramatically influences our capacity to lead, and therefore we have written this book explicitly exploring connections between architecture and leadership. It is our constant contact with and habitation of architecture, in virtually every aspect of our lives, and the constant presence and influence of the principles that lie therein, that make architecture the perfect instructor as we explore a new way, anchored on the sound principles of our history. Therefore, architecture is not something that one would have to go somewhere new to see or read something new to discover. Architecture is, however, something that we need to see anew, which is to understand it more thoroughly, inhabit it more intentionally, embrace it more openly, and learn from it more knowingly. Before turning to a detailed discussion of architecture, we begin with distinguishing what we mean when we use the terms space and place, including how our built environment influences a person's identity, meaning, and sense of purpose.

References

Churchill, W. (1943, October 28). *House of Commons Rebuilding*. London, House of Commons *393*, cc403–473. https://api.parliament.uk/historic-hansard/commons/1943/oct/28/house-of-commons-rebuilding

Collaborative on Health and the Environment. (n.d.). *Built environment*. www.healthandenvironment.org/environmental-health/environmental-risks/built-environment

Day, C. (2014). *Places of the soul: Architecture and environmental design as healing art* (3rd ed.). Routledge.

Forster, K. W. (1999). Why are some buildings more interesting than others? *Harvard Design Magazine*, *7*. www.harvarddesignmagazine.org/issues/7/why-are-some-buildings-more-interesting-than-others

Goldhagen, S. (2020). *Welcome to your world: How the built environment shapes our lives*. Harper.

Gorringe, T. (2002). *A theology of the built environment: Justice, empowerment, redemption*. Cambridge University Press.

Kant, I., & Smith, N. K. (2003). *Critique of pure reason* (Rev. 2nd ed.). Palgrave Macmillan.

Lane, B. M. (2016). Review: Albert Speer: Architecture 1932–1942. *Journal of the Society of Architectural Historians, 75*(2), 224–225. https://doi.org/10.1525/jsah.2016.75.2.224

Mackin, J. R. (1997). *Understanding the social fabric of urban communities and its relationship to prosocial behavior* (Unpublished doctoral dissertation). Michigan State University.

Merriam-Webster. (n.d.). Architecture. In *Merriam-Webster.com dictionary.* www.merriam-webster.com/dictionary/architecture

O'Donohue, J. (2000). *Eternal echoes: Celtic reflections on our yearning to belong.* Harper.

Short, J. F. (1984). The Social Fabric at risk: Toward the social transformation of risk analysis. *American Sociological Review, 49*(6), 711–725. https://doi.org/10.2307/2095526

2   Built Environment as a Place of Identity, Meaning, and Purpose

Introduction

Space and place are words or concepts we live with daily, either consciously or unconsciously, as represented by our built environment. Defining each can be elusive but important in the way that distinctions between space and place influence us. We desire for our organizations to reside in places in that when spaces become places, a person associates those places with memory, meaning, and a distinct character. Per philosopher Bollnow and geographer Tuan, there is little exploration of concretely lived space, in part because these spaces are often taken for granted (Bollnow, 1961, p. 31; Bollnow et al., 2011, p. 15; Tuan, 1977, p. 3). Their observation suggests a need to overtly consider architecture in relationship to leadership.

For some, paper maps may seem archaic, given our ubiquitous use of map applications on our phones to figure out where we are in relation to where we want to go, including the directions for getting there. We now think spatially in the way we readily associate place with a set of geo-spatial mathematical coordinates. Bollnow et al. (2011), however, contrasted mathematical space with experienced space, indicating that mathematics ignores human/space interaction (p. 18). Experienced space refers to those spaces inhabited by people and the social and relational characteristics that a space represents. Thinking solely in terms of mathematical space ignores and potentially minimizes and dehumanizes the lived experiences of place.

Space can be described as abstract and undifferentiated, whereas place is familiar, context-specific, meaning rich, and endowed with value (Jacobsen, 2012, p. 55; Tuan, 1977, p. 73). These ideas are tricky to define, but we seem to intuitively know the difference between space and place. If I say, this is a cool place, or that person invades my space, you know of which I speak. Yet, there must be more definitive ways to distinguish space and place. Bollnow et al. (2011) identified qualities of experienced space as areas or locations with qualitative differences, including rich

DOI: 10.4324/9781003166788-2

content and value. The purpose of this chapter is to explore space, place, and architecture as spatial, experienced, and communicators of values. Spatiality, wherein a person's physical body exists in space, is a place to start.

Spatiality

I am here. You are there. Humans are embodied spatial beings. The idea that I cannot be in two places at once can be a frustrating acknowledgment! And yet, we can seamlessly move between private and public, from here to there. Space was described in various ways, including that which surrounds us, elbow room, freedom of movement, nonconstricting, shared, the distance between objects, making or clearing a space, and a form of organizing (Marcel as cited in Bollnow et al., 2011, p. 37; Tuan, 1977). Many expressions illustrate these descriptions: *This room is spacious, give me some space, don't crowd me* or *don't invade my space, make some space.* Space as embodied simply means that we are physical beings within a single space at a time and that this embodiment is how we move within and between spaces. In this sense, space is not solely physical, although certainly physical elements of the built environment contribute to our sense of the available space within which we move and act.

Spatial influences are perceived experiences of what is possible. With individuals, desired personal space varies from person to person due to culture, gender, height, weight, and a host of factors. Personal space is that space around a person which is theirs; it denotes safety, security, and freedom of movement. Personal space is a vulnerable space such that if someone invades our space, we may feel threatened and react with *get out of my face.* To experience an invasion of space denotes a personal experience of physical, personal, and social violation.

Places are specific and serve as definers of space. Our dailiness transports us to many places such as work, the grocery, retail stores, restaurants, parks, etc. I say I'm going to X, where X is the specific place, I plan to go. We realize in our expression of going that we will pass many places along the way and encounter others in so doing. Public places are unique in their potential for diversity and the coexistence of strangers. Jacobsen (2003), who holds a PhD in theology and culture, asserted, "Public places facilitate incidental contact and relationships with people we know and don't know and spaces for conversation" (pp. 81–83). In this sense, public places can facilitate the "formation of informal relationships and the building up of existing relationships" (Jacobsen, p. 79). Our movement within public places is not solely utilitarian but social, opportune for interaction.

Experienced Space

People exist within a particular location filled with meaning, attachment, a sense of belonging, and rootedness. These elements afford places of experience, history, and collective and individual identity. People assign meaning to places. According to environmental psychologists Proshansky et al. (1983), "Through personal attachment to geographically locatable locations, a person acquires a sense of belonging and purpose which give meaning" (p. 59). Attachment is related to one's sense of rootedness and belonging, a sense of placement and inclusion in the dailiness of life. Cresswell, Professor of History and International Affairs at Northeastern University (2004), noted, "When humans invest meaning in a portion of space and then become attached to it in some way it becomes a place" (p. 10).

For example, on Friday nights, my husband and I (Alicia) would often go to our locally owned restaurant, sit at the bar, have dinner, converse with whoever was there, laugh, and share life with our neighbors. We affectionately thought of this as our place. The place was more than a space for eating; it was a place for neighbors to share life in community. In his study on British pub life, Oldenburg (1999) described the pub as an example of spaces that became places where the practice of going there represented a movement from solely physical to include the social and communal aspects of life. When these places disappear, a person can experience a sense of grief or loss. A feeling of rootedness combined with a sense of absence when places are gone may contribute to feelings of crisis, given that a person needs firm ground underfoot (Bollnow et al., 2011, p. 23). Individuals may be decentered or disoriented with a loss of home because the home defines who and what they are in terms of strong affective ties to locale (Proshansky et al., 1983, p. 61).

By considering home as the most fundamental of places, we begin to understand the power of all the subsequent places we inhabit. Home is the central area of concern for a person's sense of identity, belonging, rootedness, and experience of dwelling. Home is a personal, intimate place, representative of our sense of self. Home represents "multiple meanings and significance, memories, refuge, and independence" (Lashley & Morrison, 2000, p. 103). We talk about our heart home, a feeling of hominess that touches the very core of our identity. To tell a guest to make yourself at home is a big deal because you are sharing your most intimate space with a stranger. Home as a private space represents refuge, shelter, a place of nurture and recovery, and ownership. We speak in terms of our home as the place where we live. In terms of going home, our sense of home can vary proximally. For example, if I'm in Europe, I mean going home to mean returning to the United States; if in Tennessee, I mean a return to Phoenix;

when in the Phoenix airport, let's go home refers distinctly to my home, the place where I live privately. All these home places contribute to a sense of identity, belonging, and a sense of rootedness.

Understanding the intersection of home and organizations raises in importance as we consider the effects of organizational changes and the nature of work related to pandemics such as Covid-19. A result of the Covid-19 pandemic was a blurring of place identity between work and home. Home became the central domain of all life despite lacking the affordances typically associated with our offices or organizations. This reallocation has disrupted our understanding of the once clear roles of home versus work and of those two common places versus various third places, referred to by Oldenburg, where we gather to intentionally separate from those more common places. The lostness and unease resulting from this disruption requires a new understanding and appreciation for what our built environments will mean going forward.

In part, a person's experienced space requires four things: making a home, avoiding isolation in a person's inner space, inclusion in public life exterior to one's home, and having trust in the greater space (Bollnow et al., 2011, p. 288). Those displaced from the workplace or home experience disorientation expressed through statements like: *I'm not welcome there*; *I don't feel like I can be myself there*; *I can't go back there*, etc. Spaces become places as people live, work, become attached, and assign meaning.

Because of these attachments and meanings, each place holds expected social norms, values, and expectations. Place identities is the term coined by Proshansky et al. (1983) to describe differing uses and experiences within place along with the corresponding variations in the social meaning, values, and ideas. For example, comparing a sports arena with a funeral home, the physical design suggests specific affordances along with social norms and expected behaviors, given the place, purpose, and nature of interaction. Places' social definitions consist of norms, behaviors, rules, and regulations inherent in the use of these places. In this regard, places enact a regulatory effect in their suggestion of appropriate behaviors and actions. These perceived social norms suggest what should happen, what the setting should be like, and how others should behave (Proshansky et al., 1983, pp. 67, 69). For example, walking into a wedding suggests very different behaviors than walking into a funeral or attending a football game. We know how to act and what is expected given the physical place and event. So too, with organizational design, the built environment projects affordances, triggering expected movement, relationships, behaviors, and interactions. Over time, people's experiences within a place create a shared history and suite of associated memories.

Collective and individual memory contributes to our capacity to assign meaning, history, and eventfulness to a place. We build memorials, plaques,

Figure 2.1 Close up of the 911 Memorial, which marks the locations of the former World Trade Center buildings, New York City, NY. From: Thomas Eidsvold, unsplash.com.

and statues to commemorate certain historical places or events. The 911 Memorial (Figure 2.1) is an example of a memorial designed to physically link the past to the present while crafting a narrative that fosters memories and reflection.

Places hold significance in the way they provide visual and physical cues and physicality to significant life events. We remember a place based on our experiences there, for better or worse. Placelessness is detrimental to identity and memory (Jacobsen, 2012, p. 57). French anthropologist Marc Augé (2008) went so far as to assert that "If a place can be defined as relational, historical, or concerned with identity, then a space which cannot be defined as relational, historical, or concerned with identity is a nonplace" (p. 63). Nonplaces are merely spaces of circulation, consumption, and communication (Auge, p. viii). The built environment contributes to or commemorates the history and culture of a place and human activities within it.

Architecture, Space, and Place

Architecture is called the "mother of all arts" (Pierre et al., 2015). Creating and arranging our physical environment was one of the first accomplishments of humankind. Throughout history, architecture was and continues to be the rare endeavor that surrounds all of us, materially affecting each of us, every day of our lives, impacting our lives in a way that very few disciplines can claim. Humans all over the world are born, live, work, worship, and are educated, entertained, and healed within a built environment, within the embrace of architecture. Humanity exists within architecture, finding identity, meaning, and purpose within architectural spaces that become meaningful places. When you consider architecture's influence on humans, connections between architecture and leadership rise in importance, speaking to the enormous potential and effect that architecture has on how we live in the world and the quality of life we enjoy. Goldhagen (2020) put it this way:

> To say the built environment **is** us is but a slight exaggeration. And it is certainly no exaggeration to say that the built environment shapes who we are and how we move through the world physically, socially and cognitively, as well as in the sense of how we construct and reconstruct our identity.
>
> (p. 85)

When we speak of architecture, it may be tempting to think of architecture as an object, as only something to look at, that only a select few get to see or fully experience, or that architecture is someone else's domain to consider.

We may be prone to unhelpful comparisons after experiencing great architectural design. For example, after visiting the Palace at Versailles or Hearst Castle in San Simeon, California, our homes may appear less impressive; upon seeing Apple Park in Cupertino, California (Figure 4.3), our office cubicle may seem less vibrant; or after seeing Notre Dame Cathedral in Paris, our local church may seem bland. The purpose of highlighting this thinking is to foster an expansive view of what architecture is and its place in our lives. The architecture surrounding us all day, every day, dramatically influences how we see, function within, and understand our world, including what to expect from our world and even our sense of hopefulness and possibility. Drawing upon Cresswell (2004), "Place is not just a thing in the world but a way of understanding the world" (p. 11).

The built environment constantly elicits reactions, encouraging, depressing, or inspiring us, speaking to us in many ways. Architecture's influence begins with our earliest experiences of the places in which we lived. Twentieth-century French philosopher Gaston Bachelard (2014) spoke of how this begins to unfold when he said in the book *Poetics of Space* that the "house is our corner of the world. As has often been said, it is our first universe, a real cosmos in every sense of the word." This idea of home then continues to act as an anchor point connecting us to our histories that have made us who we are. In his book, *The Architecture of Happiness*, author Alain de Botton (2006) said, "Over the years, its owners have returned [to their first home] from periods of time away and, on looking around them, remembered who they were" (p. 11). Country singer Miranda Lambert (2010) refers to this same idea in her song *The House That Built Me* when she sings, "I thought if I could touch this place or feel it, the brokenness inside of me might start healing." Regardless of how far we roam and how much digital space becomes part of our lives, the solid foundation of home continues to beckon.

In his essay, *Towards an Architecture of Humility*, Finnish architect Juhani Pallasmaa (1998) said, "In an age of simulation and virtual reality, we still long for a home." As a signifier of place, architecture, exemplified by our dwellings, works as a potent reminder, a holder of memories and connections. As significant as this work of reminding is, somehow the places in which we abide do more than this. They interact with us and even speak to us of where we started, how far we've come, and where we might go. American humorist Mark Twain (1917) said of his house in Hartford, Connecticut:

> To us our house was not unsentient matter – it had a heart and a soul and eyes to see us with, and approvals and solicitudes and deep sympathies, & lived in its grace & in the peace of its benediction. We never came home from an absence that its face did not light up & speak out its eloquent welcome – & we could not enter it unmoved.

Twain alludes to the greater role of architecture throughout our lives and to an important insight about the ability of architecture to speak to us and communicate messages, even when we are not listening. This speaking is not only one of the unique capabilities of architecture, but also one we greatly desire and to which we are drawn.

Victorian-era art critic John Ruskin (as cited in de Botton, 2006) said, "We want two things from our buildings. We want them to shelter us. We want them to speak to us of whatever we find important and need to be reminded of." When our architecture speaks to us, it speaks as part of a whole, as a piece of its context, as a voice added to the choir of buildings all around us. As stated by Goldhagen (2020), "Buildings are choirs rather than soloists; they possess a multiple nature from which arise opportunities for beautiful consonance as well as dissension and discord" (p. 3). This collective choir sings of everything important in our lives, and this powerful conversant relationship occurs in our offices, classrooms, churches, and all the places where we spend the precious moments of our lives.

de Botton (2006) said, "Buildings speak – and on topics which are readily discerned. They speak of democracy or aristocracy, openness or arrogance, welcome or threat, a sympathy for the future or a hankering for the past" (p. 71). de Botton referred to all buildings, even the most seemingly mundane and utilitarian, because they all have the potential to become places of human experience and activity. Researchers Elsbach and Bechky (2007) said, "Places become meaningful to people through the activities or actions that have happened in them – people remember these actions and events through their spatial understanding of the location." Architecture has a profound power on our lives in a variety of ways.

Humans translate spaces into places based on their lived experiences, and this translation matters to us greatly. de Botton (2006) asked,

> Why should it matter what our environment has to say to us? Why should architects bother to design buildings which communicate specific sentiments and ideas, and why should we be so negatively affected by places which reverberate with what we take to be the wrong allusions? Why are we vulnerable, so inconveniently vulnerable, to what the spaces we inhabit are saying?
>
> (p. 106)

Architecture has much to say, whether or not we are consciously listening. Thusly, architecture directly influences leadership and the social context.

Chapter Summary

To be human . . . is to be placed (Gorringe, 2002, p. 23). The concept of dwelling moves us from the physical to the personal. Dwelling represents a point of reference, an orientation toward life and its reality. To be alienated is to be lost, to be homeless. Dwelling in this sense of place roots a person in their lived experiences, their feeling at home in the world (Gorringe, 2002, p. 24). According to Bollnow (1961), "To dwell is not an activity . . . but a [rootedness], a determination of man in which he realizes his true essence" (p. 33). This distinction between space and place is critical to understanding fully what is at stake in our understanding of architecture. A foundational suite of principles such as time, firmness, utility, and delight contribute toward architecture being declared good.

References

Augé, M. (2008). *Non-places: Introduction to an anthropology of supermodernity*. Verso.

Bachelard, G., & Jolas, M. (2014). *The poetics of space*. Penguin Books.

Bollnow, O. F. (1961). Lived-space. *Philosophy Today*, *5*(1), 31–39. https://doi.org/10.5840/philtoday1961513

Bollnow, O. F., Shuttleworth, C., & Kohlmaier, J. (2011). *Human space*. Hyphen.

Cresswell, T. (2004). *Place: A short introduction*. Blackwell.

de Botton, A. (2006). *The architecture of happiness*. Penguin Books.

Elsbach, K. D., & Bechky, B. A. (2007). It's more than a desk: Working smarter through leveraged office design. *California Management Review*, *49*(2), 80–101. https://doi.org/10.2307/41166384

Goldhagen, S. (2020). *Welcome to your world: How the built environment shapes our lives*. Harper.

Gorringe, T. (2002). *A theology of the built environment: Justice, empowerment, redemption*. Cambridge University Press.

Jacobsen, E. O. (2003). *Sidewalks in the Kingdom: New urbanism and the Christian faith*. Brazos Press.

Jacobsen, E. O. (2012). *The space between: A Christian engagement with the built environment*. Baker Academic.

Lambert, M. (2010). *The House that built me* [song]. On Revolution. Blackbird Studios.

Lashley, C., & Morrison, A. J. (2000). *In search of hospitality: Theoretical perspectives and debates*. Butterworth-Heinemann.

Oldenburg, R. (1999). *The great good place: Cafés, coffee shops, bookstores, bars, hair salons, and other hangouts at the heart of a community*. Marlowe.

Pallasmaa, J. (1998). *Toward an architecture of humility*. www.geocities.ws/mitchellmosesstudio/pallasmaa01.pdf

Pierre, C., Normand, J., & Cordingley, R. A. (2015). *Orders of architecture*. Dover Publications.

Proshansky, H. M., Fabian, A. K., & Kaminoff, R. (1983). Place-identity: Physical world socialization of the self. *Journal of Environmental Psychology*, *3*, 57–83. https://doi.org/10.1016/s0272-4944(83)80021-8

Tuan, Y. (1977). *Space and place: The perspective of experience*. University of Minnesota Press.

Twain, M., & Paine, A. B. (1917). *Mark Twain's letters*. Harper & Brothers.

3 Defining Architecture as "Good"

Introduction

Not only is architecture an influential constant in our daily lives, it is also a thing that draws us to visit and explore the great cities of the world. In fact, it is often the most visible element representative of a city's identity. When we go to New York, Paris, Moscow, or Beijing, we are really going to see the Empire State Building, the Eiffel Tower (Figure 3.1), Red Square, or the Forbidden City.

It is the significant, meaningful, and historic architecture that makes those cities worthy destinations. It is largely, in fact, the architecture of a city that most typically gives residents of that city pride of place. This is one of the ways in which architecture is *good*. We are all drawn to the power and presence of good buildings wherever we find them because they remind us, they hold memories of experiences, they speak to us, and they shape us. The purpose of this chapter is to explore those formative aspects of architecture which contribute to the design being declared good, such as time, firmness, utility, and delight.

Architecture's Powers of Creative Formation

Architecture is an academic pursuit, a licensed profession, and often a high-minded topic of consideration in discussions, films, books, and articles. At its essence, though, the architecture that continually surrounds us is simply the artistic formulation of functional space – big, small, grand, or ordinary, including all aspects of a space's design. This means that architecture encompasses the formulation of exterior spaces, interior spaces, rooms, public and private spaces, buildings, landscapes, and even urban design, using the intentional employment of materials, natural elements, texture, color, shape, and light. Whether we are cognizant of architecture or not, this artistic formulation of the spaces and places around us contributes

DOI: 10.4324/9781003166788-3

Figure 3.1 The iconic Eiffel Tower, Paris, France. From Maria Wachala/Moment via Getty Images.

and communicates clearly and powerfully. This is architecture's influential nature and potential for good.

It is true to say that many things besides architecture can have this kind of positive influence. Every creative effort we experience potentially and powerfully influences and shapes how we see the world. In the creative world alone, music, art, design, film, photography, literature, and other creative efforts surround and affect our lives. However, there is a big difference between most human creative expressions and that of architecture. Goldhagen (2020) stated that "the built environment shapes our lives and the choices we make in all the ways that these other arts do – combined" (p. XIV).

In the book *Conversations with Goethe in the Last Years of His Life*, German poet, playwright, and novelist Johann Wolfgang von Goethe (as cited in Goethe et al., 1839) said: "I call architecture frozen music." And we can see that music is like architecture in many ways, such as the repetitive cadence and rhythm of the structure, and the harmonious melding of the individual notes and parts into a cohesive whole, including the emotional response of crescendo and decrescendo. However, music is a creative expression that exists within, translated into hearing and vibrations, experienced and translated as the music moves through your body, mind, and soul. But this experience of music only happens when you are listening to it. One's experience with art, film, or literature is similarly a process of bringing something into yourself from the outside, but only temporarily while one is in dialogue with those elements. Goldhagen (2020) said to:

> Think of how listening to your favorite piece of music can change your mood. How looking at an excellent painting transports you into another world. How an unusually shaped piece of furniture makes you muse upon the human body in repose; a dance performance activates thoughts of your own body in motion. Successful sculptures can incite imaginings of standing tall or slithering or floating; good film imbues our lives with story lines and dramas. Each of these arts affects us in ways that are powerful and real, but each does so only when we actively engage it. Usually that is only for a short time on any given day, and many days not at all.
>
> (p. xiv)

Music is a creative expression that exists within you and moves you, for a time. Uniquely, with architecture, you physically go inside of it, processing the experience while you move through it. Our experiences with architecture as described persist consistently throughout our lives. Rare is the moment when one doesn't find themselves inside, next to, or somehow in sight of architecture. Moreover, if that architecture is designed well, it will inhabit you spiritually and emotionally while you inhabit it physically. As you move through space, the architecture will move you. And conversely, if designed poorly, the architecture you move through and inhabit will sap your energy, depress and discourage you, dulling your ability to be inspired and to experience happiness, as noted by de Botton (2006).

> Architectural design is both art and science where the architect translates ethos, culture, history, and functionality into an appropriate design. As the architect moves from functional needs to conceptual design, their translation represents the hopes and aspirations of those who will use the space.

From Abstraction to Habitability

Artists take the real world and make it abstract. Architects take something abstract; a feeling, a principle, an idea, and make it into something real, something habitable. This quality of habitation distinguishes architecture, given that other artistic mediums generally do not require habitation as one of the required design elements. This habitation of architecture provides a sensory full-body experience. Barrie (1996) stated, "Architectural form and space is not apprehended by sight only. The smell of materials, inhabitant, food, surroundings; the feel and texture of materials and surfaces, the sound of echoes and footsteps are all part of the complete architectural experience" (p. 47). Tuan (1977) emphasized how architecture continues to "exert a direct impact on the senses and feeling. The body responds . . . to such basic features of design." The achievement and subsequent habitation of architecture not only can but also always does materially affect human outcomes.

If done well, architecture can enhance our relationships, increase productivity, inspire learning, improve health, and even, as argued by urban theorist Jane Jacobs (1992) in *The Death and Life of Great American Cities*, enrich communities and decrease crime. If done poorly and unintentionally, our architecture can result in outcomes much more negative and dire. As stated in *The Architecture of Community*, Krier et al. (2009) noted:

> In the same way that people, objects, or landscape can by their sheer presence fill your heart with joy or rob it of all energy, so can buildings make or break your day. For buildings are never neutral, however neutral or insipid they look. They act positively or negatively upon you; they enrich or impoverish your life in a radical way.

For example, in Disney's animated movie *Zootopia* (Howard et al., 2016), all the story's characters were depicted by a representative animal, and the film's Department of Motor Vehicles (DMV) workers were portrayed as sloths, a negative stereotypical perception of DMV employees. Drawing upon historical perceptions of a typical DMV work environment as monotone, boring, and bland, you might begin to believe that these workers (and many others in similar circumstances) have been sentenced to this fate, having no other choice or chance. It is interesting to see the ways that these workers valiantly alter their environment by adding flowers, balloons, knickknacks, or pictures of their family, artifacts designed to reflect personality and esthetic beauty. All of these are efforts to add something – anything, to try to bring some life and hope to their physical environment. Architecture gives us a choice and a chance, the effects of which need to be recognized and intentionally considered. We need our architecture to be good.

We have previously spoken of how architecture becomes a vital component and shaper of our collective social fabric, affecting our culture and lived experiences. We see examples of this influence continually playing out in the world around us. For example, nearly every football stadium in the country has some version of a tunnel that players run through to access

Figure 3.2 Football player emerging from the darkness of a stadium tunnel into the light of the playing field. From: Brocreative, shutterstock.com.

the playing field. These tunnels (Figure 3.2), as exemplified at traditional college football powers like Notre Dame, the University of Oklahoma, and the University of Southern California, are special places and meaningful parts of the game experience. One runs through a long, dark, constraining, echoing passageway, often ceremonially touching or otherwise paying homage to a passage written over the exit or some other icon, and then suddenly emerges into a huge, brightly lit, roaring stadium full of fans. Joey Getherall (as cited in und.com, n.d.), a former football player at Notre Dame, said,

> I can honestly say the greatest athletic moment of my life was running out of the tunnel my freshman year . . . it gives you chills . . . I almost started crying . . . No one can understand what it feels like until they run out the tunnel.

What Getherall experienced running out of that tunnel was a multi-sensory life experience, a part of the social fabric of his life and that of the fans watching him, all provided by the design of the building in which he went to work.

What becomes clear is that our experience of buildings is more than physical. Architecture affects us through every one of our senses and even our

Figure 3.3 Cutaway View of the Tabernacle of Moses Showing the Procession of Sensory Elements. Some content taken from The Tabernacle pamphlet by Rose Publishing. Copyright © 2006, 2013. Used by permission of Hendrickson Rose Publishing Group, represented by Tyndale House Publishers. All rights reserved.

psyche. A stadium tunnel, a simple passageway designed to efficiently move a large group of large people from their locker rooms to the playing field can facilitate that kind of visceral, emotional effect. An intentionally designed space must be able to do so even more effectively. This is the power of architecture; the way humans assign meaning to the spaces they inhabit.

This power of architecture to shape our social fabric through intentionally holistic experience is on display in examples throughout history. The Mosaic Tabernacle (Figure 3.3), described in the biblical Old Testament, was a structure designed around this idea of fully engaging the inhabitant. Every step through the tabernacle was thoroughly planned to achieve ever deeper levels of physical and spiritual cleanliness and preparation, separating one further from the darkness and filth of the world and moving one closer to the light and perfection of God.

Some 3500 years later, legendary American Architect Louis Kahn employed a version of this idea in his entry sequence for the Kimbell Art Museum (Figure 3.4) in Fort Worth, Texas.

Kahn intended for visitors to pass across a quiet grass lawn, over crunching gravel, past gurgling fountains, under a grove of low trees, and up a short flight of stairs. When the visitor has traversed and experienced these elements, they become effectively visually, aurally, and experientially separated from the sight and sound of the city from whence they recently

Figure 3.4 Entry sequence Kimbell Art Museum, Fort Worth, TX. Photo by Mark A. Roberson.

departed to engage in this journey. This was what Kahn believed was needed to prepare one physically and emotionally to view great art.

We see this same pursuit of using architecture to intentionally shape, for better or worse, how we experience our lives in larger-scale applications as well. The Congress for the New Urbanism (n.d.) promotes urban environments that create a better, healthier quality of life. Albert Speer designed multiple buildings around Germany and even proposed a redesign of the entire city of Berlin expressly to promote the philosophies of Hitler and the Third Reich, preparatory for residents and visitors to embrace those philosophies fully.

So, architecture is more than just space design and construction. It is also more than the obviously impressive civic, cultural, recreational, and religious landmarks we admire. Our collective social fabric is genuinely dependent on the successfully built realization of an idea, concept, or greater purpose communicating the ethos and values of the architect and those for whom the structure is designed. Goldhagen (2020) said, "The leaders of the cognitive revolution reveal – perhaps mostly inadvertently – that our built environments are the instruments on which this orchestra of our senses plays its music" (p. 38). The act of identifying why we need a building (e.g., a place to live, work, play, watch sports, worship God, engage with art, etc.) is merely the starting point for expressing purpose from which an architect begins to conceive a conceptual design. Architecture is about so much more than function; it is about ideas that shape the fabric of our lives. The purposes of these ideas and their eventual built manifestations have varied dramatically throughout history, but this primary relationship between architecture and its shaping idea has been constant.

Layered onto purpose are things like individual, organizational, and community identity, history, culture, mission, values, and perceptions of how a building symbolically communicates your vision. As architectural design moved past its most utilitarian aims of function, shelter, and protection into more symbolic and meaningful typologies, the ultimate result of this formulating relationship represented the values and character of those who built these places, aspiring to achieve a specific end effect on the users and observers. Referring to John Ruskin, the Bible, and Albert Speer, as well as other examples, while buildings were originally designed to shelter us, very quickly architecture's power was realized – the power to speak. People recognized their ability to leverage architecture's voice for greater purposes. These purposes had many motives and manifestations throughout history. Yet it is this power to speak and communicate greater purpose that must be explored, learned, and understood to intentionally leverage architecture as a powerful and influential part of leadership.

Good or Bad Architecture

Architecture can be assessed in terms of whether it is good or bad. We are faced with the question of whether Margaret Wolfe Hungerford's (1878) assertion is true when in *Molly Bawn* she claimed that "beauty is in the eye of the beholder." Making judgments about the relative goodness or badness of something so seemingly subjective is often an uncomfortable exercise in that so many relative elements seem to go into one's understanding and experience of those qualities. You may have heard someone say *I don't know much about art but I know what I like*, or *I know it when I see it*. These clichés are popular for a reason. We regularly embrace canons of recognized greatness in all aspects of life, be it in the realms of literature, art, music, theology, or many others. For example, *Anna Karenina*, by venerated Russian author Leo Tolstoy, is understood to be great literature as opposed to a romance novel at the airport bookstore. Professor and author William Saunders (1999) said, in his essay *From Taste to Judgment*:

For the Pope, there are canonical scriptures and doctrines which define Catholicism . . .. For F.R. Leavis, and many literary critics, there was a canonic Great Tradition of literature that always needed asserting, upholding and reevaluating by those of supposed superior sensibility.

(p. 52)

It is then important to think similarly about concepts of good versus bad architecture. Architecture, like so many other human endeavors, is something that we can understand as good or bad based on widely accepted characteristics or criteria. Saunders (1999) went on to say:

> The attempt to avoid forming judgements about architecture in the name of relativism, anti-elitist, distaste for presumptuousness, epistemological skepticism, or simple indifference leads only to self-contradiction (for one does judge anyway) and to aimlessness and egocentrism. It is absurd to argue about preferences, it is absurd not to argue about judgements.

So, the effort to understand a basis upon which to be able to judge and create effective and meaningful physical environments is legitimate. It seems that much like great leadership, great architecture seems hard to define, but we know it when we see and experience it. However, our judgments of architecture always go deeper than image or style for those who see it – architecture has to work for those who use it. So, forming such a framework around architecture might be easier than it is for most artistic endeavors in that architecture is, in this significant way, fundamentally different, with added dimensions that help quickly establish a minimum baseline for consideration. Saunders (1999) said,

> Yet, despite the from-the-gut strength, even dominance, of personal interests and preferences in the evaluation of architecture, architecture, unlike, say, sculpture, quickly forces acknowledgement of multiple, less-personal criteria – agreement prevails that buildings should protect us from harsh weather and meet the functional and programmatic needs of the clients.

(p. 132)

Saunders is saying that there is an easily identifiable, minimum baseline of acceptable quality for architecture that simply doesn't exist in any other creative endeavor. To understand how some buildings move past this minimum baseline, we can look to what is commonly accepted as the canon of the greatest and most important architecture throughout world history and recognize in that canon many commonalities and similar characteristics.

Fundamental principles can be identified as essential to not only discerning, but also to making great architecture. Italian designer Massimo Vignelli (as cited in Hustwit, 2007) said in the documentary film *Helvetica*, "The life of a designer is one of fight: fight against the ugliness." A framework can be built upon which to not only judge the relative merits of architecture, but also to fight against the ugliness and to better understand how to intentionally formulate spaces and places that are meaningful, significant, and contributory to leadership strategy. Architecture that comes to be known as great is architecture that endures beyond its time and context.

Test of Time

The historical canon of great works of architecture is filled with buildings that are a product of their specific context – the physical conditions, climate, economy, theology, politics, culture, and everything that existed in that place and time that shaped their design and making. Timeless architecture is often misunderstood as designed to echo or mimic a time other than its own. However, the history of great architecture teaches us that timeless architecture is always a product of its own time, done well enough to continue to have power and meaning beyond its time. So, to be considered great, architecture must be able to stand the test of time. Buildings, as well as music, literature, and art held in high esteem over an extended period, are those that we hold forth as great. Although forgotten buildings, music, literature, and art are not necessarily bad, those that create a stir when they are new yet quickly fade from the discussion are typically not considered great. Architecture that stands the test of time does not have to adhere to a particular style or create a buzz for its audacity, newness, or wow-factor, although it can do all those things. It is typically, however, architecture that is recognizable as founded on its context in some meaningful way, designed for long-term appreciation and quality, using widely held, time-tested principles of design.

We must avoid the tendencies to overvalue current things or undervalue the lessons that time provides us. Authors Shoup and Hinrichs (2020), in their book *Literature and Leadership*, pointed out that author and academic C.S. Lewis believed "that people of any generation suffer a sort of blindness from being surrounded by only current ideas and philosophies and largely ignorant, or hostile to, past or future ideas or assumptions." We must be willing to weigh the good we see in the new against the lessons we've learned from all that has come before. The American Institute of Architecture (AIA) recognizes these competing values by not only awarding prizes for the design of new buildings each year, but also by awarding the Twenty-five Year Award to buildings that have gained or held great respect over at least the past quarter century. According to the AIA (n.d.), "The Twenty-five Year Award showcases buildings that set a precedent . . . stood the test of time for 25–35 years and continues to set standards of excellence for its architectural design and significance." William Saunders (1999) stated that, "Appreciation of the sensory qualities of architecture requires slowness and patience" (p. 101). Saunders (1999) went on to describe how "[Finnish modernist architect] Alvar Aalto believed that the value of a building is best judged fifty years after completion." In *The 7 Lamps of Architecture*, John Ruskin (1907) spoke of this long-view of architecture when he said, "Therefore, when we build, let us think that we build forever. Let it not be for present delight, nor for present use alone" (LE note 1, p. 233). Architecture that stands the test of time is architecture that is good.

In identifying these buildings considered great over time, we can also then identify and understand common characteristics giving them that standing. In understanding these characteristics, we can hope to shape effective and meaningful spaces for the organizations we lead today and tomorrow. To build a foundation for this understanding, we will explore some of the first such characteristics ever recorded, those of firmness, utility, and delight.

Firmness, Utility, and Delight

Somewhere around 15–30 BC, a Roman architect named Marcus Vitruvius Pollio laid out his framework for great architecture. He wrote what is widely considered the first known and most famous text in the history of architecture, landscape design, engineering, and town planning, and the only book of its kind to survive from antiquity. Vitruvius' (1960) *De Architectura*, translated into English as *Ten Books on Architecture*, has survived many rediscoveries and rewritings over the centuries. In his *Ten Books*, Vitruvius laid out his treatise on, among other things, architecture, engineering, armaments, wells, aqueducts, the planets, and machinery. Specifically, in Book One, he expounds on a three-component structure upon which he asserts that great architecture is dependent. This widely known and historically enduring pronouncement of Vitruvius' tome is that architecture provides "firmitas, utilitas, and venustas," commonly translated as firmness, utility, and delight. Vitruvius' ancient statement puts forward three very different yet, according to Vitruvius, all-encompassing ideas about architecture. Vitruvius' exact meaning in his choice of words and the intent of these ideas have been interpreted differently throughout the two millennia since they were written, so we will briefly examine each of these ideas individually.

Firmness

Firmness refers to the qualities of a building that are solid, permanent, and physical. Thought of in this way, firmness is a quality common to almost every building throughout history. We know a building cannot be considered a success if it is not solidly built and lacks lasting attributes. The basic foundation for all understanding and meaning of architectural built form, in fact, can be thought of as firmness. This is a huge part of the baseline qualification for good architecture spoken of by William Saunders. But it also speaks to the idea of timelessness.

As noted, architecture was one of the first endeavors of humankind. As civilizations began to take form, people realized very quickly the value not only of individual shelter, but also of meeting, working, worshipping, and socializing corporately, as exemplified by examples such as ancient Mesopotamia, Egypt, and China. The architecture of our world literally traces the history of humanity – our technological capacity, our belief systems, and our world views. As we look historically at things built and left behind, we realize that architecture tells us who we were, who we are, and who we can become. Architecture, as Vitruvius (1960) said, has firmness. It takes a long time to accomplish, and it often lasts a long time when done. Architecture is one of humanity's most time, energy, and resource-intensive endeavors. Gothic cathedrals, for example, sometimes took hundreds of years to finish. And then architecture, once constructed, lasts for centuries, or even millennia. There are structures still standing on our earth that are as old as human civilization, such as Tell Qaramel (±10,000 BC), Gobekli Tepe (±9,000 BC), and Catalhoyuk (±7,000 BC) (Figure 4.2). Architecture is indeed a forever endeavor.

It follows then that in a hundred years or a thousand years, people will look at our current buildings and realize who we were, what we could accomplish, and what we valued in the early 21st century. So, great architecture must be that which takes such a long view of history, meaning, and functional life. Architecture must be able to physically withstand time and carry its ethos or meaning well past the lifespan of its creators. Even though great architecture must serve its purpose and, in Vitruvius (1960) words, have utility, it is not solely derived from pursuing the most utilitarian or expedient solution, the cheapest, or the easiest to accomplish. Architectural design is about making decisions based on firm principles, historical information, the context, and what will stand the test of time by best serving people and users for generations to come.

Utility

The term utility is somewhat self-evident in that a building should be useful, successfully serve its purpose, be buildable, and practical. A building can be firm and, in some ways, delightful but ultimately unsuccessful if proven impractical for use. An important consideration of this idea of utility is how one strategizes the use of space, from the application of liturgy in a worship space to the arrangement of tables in a conference room. Utility also involves ideas of being doable, practical, and economically feasible.

Utility, in its many forms and meanings, is vital to successfully completing and using architectural projects. The great Pyramids of Giza were certainly an exercise in firmness, as they have lasted for over 4,500 years and are the only surviving member of the seven wonders of the ancient world. However, they weren't built just to stand and last or even just to be impressive icons, but to serve the vital function of ushering a dead pharaoh into his afterlife destiny as a god. Such massive efforts as these had to have meaningful and critical purposes to make them worthwhile, lest the efforts dedicated to their making be wasted. So, in architecture, the work must be done as a proper response to its context, and with due consideration for and affordances related to the ultimate purpose of the building (what activities will be carried out within the building), the available budget, the availability of materials and labor, etc. Basic usability and functionality, utility, is another piece of achieving Saunders' (1999) baseline qualification for good architecture.

Delight

Delight points to this ability for our spaces and places to be and accomplish more than many of us previously imagined and to be more important and influential than many of us previously understood. The term delight differs from firmness or utility in that it is a term that is less self-evident and refers to qualities that are much more elusive in many ways. Qualities of delight are not necessary for a building to be firm or functional, and a quick survey of the built environment around us reveals that much of it is indeed firm and serves its utilitarian function without any qualities of delightfulness at all.

For a building to ascend to the more meaningful level of delight, it must begin by being both firm and useful. In an interview, Juhani Pallasmaa (as cited in Crosbie, 2021) said, "The metaphysical task of architecture is to mediate and articulate our relations with the world. Historically, this has been more significant than the utility or rationality of buildings." This pursuit of delight can even elevate spaces to the level of being considered sacred, which is an ultimate condition of delight, but not the only one. Author Eric Weiner (2012) addressed the promise of this idea of delight in a New York Times article where he referred to such special places as thin places:

> Thin places are often sacred ones – St. Peter's Basilica in Vatican City [Figure 1.1], The Blue Mosque in Istanbul – but they need not be, at least not conventionally so. A park or even a city square can be a thin place. So can an airport . . . (such as) Hong Kong international.

Weiner (2012) explained the delight in these thin places, and the real potential for their connection to leadership when he said, "Thin places relax us,
but they also transform us – or more accurately unmask us. In thin places,
we become our more essential selves." de Botton (2006) echoed this emphasis on the transformational power of delightful places:

> Belief in the significance of architecture is premised on the notion that
> we are, for better or worse, different people in different places, and on
> the notion that it is the architecture's task to render vivid to us who we
> might ideally be.

So, in this pursuit of becoming our more essential selves or who we might
ideally be, we find large and small examples where people go to great
lengths and expense to rise above firmness and utility to bring delight to
their places – the living and working environments in which they spend
their lives.

History makes clear that humans, in fact, have an innate drive to form,
effect, and curate the spaces they inhabit, to not only create more comfortable, familiar, and enjoyable places, but also to express through those places
who they are, what they believe in, hope for, and value, the delight of our
lives on this earth. The ancient cave paintings of Lascaux (Figure 3.5) in
southwestern France are examples that, as far back as we can see, humans
have desired for their spaces and places, through the employment of this

Figure 3.5 Paintings on the walls of the caves at Lascaux, France. From thipjang/
Moment via Getty Images.

idea of delight, even long before Vitruvius identified it as a formalized concept, to express their most valued accomplishments, hopes, and beliefs.

The environments resultant from this pursuit of delight become loud, albeit unvocal, leaders for people occupying those corresponding places. We see this in significant examples of iconic architecture throughout the history of built form, from the ancient Stonehenge (Figure 3.6) in Wiltshire, England, to the modern World Trade Center Transportation Hub (Figure 3.7) in New York City.

All around us, we see examples illustrating how humans personalize their physical environments. For example, my teenage daughter's bedroom decorated such that it expresses her loving horses more than oxygen, or a colleague's office adorned with photos and personal artifacts reflective of their life, or a soccer mom's vanity plates, including rear-view mirror dangles and window stickers on her bright purple minivan. These examples illustrate this drive toward delight coming through even in the face of constraining necessity. We see this drive manifest continually in our own lives in the places in which we work, learn, play, worship, recover and, in short, live our lives. Delight allows simple spaces to become places of meaning, inspiration, and attachment and is the element that differentiates between spaces that are simply firm and utilitarian and places that bring value to our lives.

Figure 3.6 The eternal mystery of Stonehenge in Wiltshire, England. From Peter Adams/DigitalVision via Getty Images.

Figure 3.7 World Trade Center Transportation Hub, New York, NY (known as the Oculus), interior of the main space and skylight. From Kyler Boone, unsplash.com.

Application to Place and Space

Consider how and where you live your life. Visualize how you move through your day. There are streets that you use solely for transportation, and streets that are destinations where you might stroll, stop, peruse, sit, and enjoy. One is a space defined by building facades, sidewalks, and curbs, while the other is a place of life, activity, and potential which draws you toward participation. You may have experienced buildings in this same way. Visualize those buildings that you frequent, such as work, grocery store, shops, the park, sports field, places of worship, etc. Some serve a utilitarian purpose, while some hold meaning and potential for life affirmation. Engagement and attachment to some places versus others is part of our human experience and determines how delightful, or how *good* we consider those places.

Our consideration of a place as good, our ability to have greater connections to and engagement with a place and to experience delight, is dependent on something existing between the person and place beyond bricks and mortar, and beyond the simple, physical elements that define space, beyond firmness and utility. Imbuing those elements with meaning depends on how they are arranged and designed to communicate meaningful messages to us of esthetics, values, purpose, and culture. Because of our resultant wish to dwell within places as opposed to just occupying them, we create memories that build more personal meaning for us, strengthening connections. Places hold symbolic value and significance in the way those places provide visual and physical cues, lending physicality to significant life events. We remember a place based on our experiences there, for better or worse. This kind of deep attachment to place becomes integrally connected to a person's identity.

Aspiring to not just define spaces in which our organizations exist, but to create good places that we identify with, feel attached to, and that are filled with delight speaks to the connection between architecture and leadership. Therefore, we see that the idea of delight is one of great and obvious importance, on which we will rely within the leadership discussion that follows.

Good Architecture is Vital to Wellbeing

So, we see why the quality of our architecture, of the places where we spend our lives, matters greatly. We feel the effects of deadened physical spaces all around us, even if we don't consciously register those feelings. We also feel architecture's effects physically, mentally, emotionally, and spiritually influencing our wellbeing, happiness, helping us to learn better, heal faster, worship more meaningfully, lifting our spirits, speaking to us by communicating values, and creating conditions for affirmation, identity formation, and a sense of belonging. In 1995, researchers Heerwagen et al. argued that physical space is contributory to poor job performance, absenteeism, employee dissatisfaction, higher turnover, and other health problems. Their research explored and emphasized the importance of humans' relationship to their architecture and physical environment. Furthermore, they argued that this built environment works along with organizational culture and values to create the environment.

Many others have studied this relationship, such as Ken Tate (2019), who believed that buildings can be healthy and that "any building . . . can be dangerous for the psyche – detrimental to one's physical and mental health" (p. 37). de Botton (2006) said that "taking architecture seriously. . . . requires that we open ourselves to the idea that we are affected by our surroundings" (p. 25). Researchers Roger Ulrich et al. (2004) studied the effects of natural light, natural views, and noise on healthcare outcomes. Huang et al. (2013) studied the intersection of architecture and public health within school environments. An approach formulated by Cannon Design, called living-centered design, was described in *The Third Teacher*, a book about how teaching and learning are linked to the physical design of a school (O'Donnell Wicklund Pigozzi and Peterson, Architects Inc., 2010). Delos and Mayo Clinic (n.d.), through the Well Living Lab, studied how indoor environments contribute to health and wellbeing within built environments. WeWork (n.d.) analyzed workplace usage and environmental impacts. Architectural space was described by Tuan (1977) as "an environment capable of affecting the people who live in it." As such, Tuan noted that architectural space can "refine human feeling and perception." French novelist Honore de Balzac (as cited in Yeazell, 2009) said,

> The events of human life, whether public or private, are so intimately linked to architecture that most observers can reconstruct nations or individuals in all the truth of their habits from the remains of their monuments or from their domestic relics.

Architect Michael Murphy explored and implemented these ideas for many years through his firm MASS Design Group as evidenced by projects such as the 2011 Butaro Hospital in Rwanda (Figure 3.8) and the 2017 African Centre of Excellence for Genomics of Infectious Diseases (ACEGID), in Nigeria.

Murphy and his firm create architecture that is designed and built specifically to heal. In a 2016 TedTalk, Murphy described how after hearing Dr. Paul Farmer discuss how hospitals make people sicker, he came to see buildings as "not simply expressive sculptures. They make visible our personal and collective aspirations as a society. Great architecture can give

Figure 3.8 Aerial view of the Butaro Hospital and surrounding context of Butaro Sector, Rwanda. From MASS Design Group.

us hope. Great architecture can heal." These examples illustrate how great architecture can be transformative.

Good Architecture has Affordances

The architectural design of working and living places typifies and thematizes expectations for the groups that inhabit them. Alfred Schutz (1962) identified typification as a dynamic by which others tacitly understand people, objects, and events based upon typical expectations, norms, and habits for groupings. For example, people have a typical understanding of what makes a cathedral a place of worship. Axiomatic to typification is thematization, the major elements of the storyline found in the typification of people, objects, and events. An example of this is how people typically spend their time in a cathedral and why a cathedral is important. In other words, the architectural design of rooms, buildings, and cities creates conditions for the development of cultures by conveying explicit and implicit messages, to which John Ruskin (as cited in de Botton, 2006) was referring when he said buildings "speak" to us. As Forster (1999) noted in his essay, *Why Are Some Buildings More Interesting Than Others*,

Other forces, chiefly invisible ones, have begun to manifest themselves through the physical properties and the experiential effects of buildings. A name for these transmitted meanings is hard to find, for they are as inseparable from the material nature and tangible qualities of a building as they are never coincident with them.

(p. 113)

This inseparable conveyed messaging is evident when people approach and walk into St. Basil's Cathedral in Moscow, the Forbidden City in Beijing, the Sydney Opera House in Sydney, Australia (Figure 3.9), the Jewish Museum in Berlin (Figure 4.9), Butaro Hospital in Rwanda (Figure 3.8), or the Rothko Chapel in Houston, to name just a few examples.

These buildings' designs clearly communicate who built them, why they were built, the conditions of their being built, and the intended expressions of culture, social expectations, and norms of those who inhabit them. We even see architecture, as employed in the overarching process of urban design, playing a significant role in this cultural messaging as exemplified in urban cores such as Los Angeles, Las Vegas, Austin, Nashville, and New York. These cities are instantly revelatory of those city's cultures, be it car culture, entertainment culture, hill country/hippie culture, country music

Figure 3.9 Sydney Opera House, Sydney, Australia, from across the harbor at night. From Tyler Duston, unsplash.com.

Figure 3.10 Lights of the Las Vegas Strip, Las Vegas, NV. From Tristan Savatier/
  Moment via Getty Images.

culture or the culture of dense, urbane urbanity. Authors and pastors Steven
Um and Justin Buzzard (2013) wrote:

> Cities are built upon the things from which humanity attempts to derive
> its ultimate significance. Whether centered around a mosque or a finan-
> cial district, a cathedral or an entertainment sector, all cities are built in
> honor of and pay homage to some type of a "god."

The human curation of spaces, places, and cities effectively conveys
these vital messages. These conveyed messages, if created and designed
intentionally, help facilitate leadership by advancing and promoting common values, enhancing organizational identity and effectiveness in all the
ways we discussed.

The desire to examine leadership through the lens of foundational elements such as the arts and humanities echoes a desire to understand leadership elements that are similarly lasting and meaningful. The desire is to
build a philosophy of leadership that will, like great architecture, outlast
the here and now and have meaning for generations to come. Architecture
as a discipline is dedicated to this intentional creation of just such effective

spaces and places, and the intentional design principles that make them effective can be appreciated and embraced by leaders and architects.

Based on the history of our architecture, buildings we care enough about to build and leave behind are not only a permanent reflection of, but are also a major shaper of, our collective history in many important ways. Understanding then the power and influence of architecture allows leaders to understand the application of space and place in the intentional promotion of culture and values. Our ability to create places that do these very things, that have these very effects on their inhabitants, that make "visible our collective aspirations as a society" (Murphy, 2016) is a very high calling and vital to our ability to live and to lead.

Chapter Summary

Architecture is an artistic endeavor and therefore open to much personal interpretation, but there are comprehensible ways to determine the value and the goodness of our built environment. Understanding these elements that can be identified as contributing to good architecture can help leaders create better built environments for their organizations. Good, intentional architecture can enable good, purposeful leadership in many ways. We propose that critical components of architecture can be articulated and include: building elements, design principles, and use strategies.

References

American Institute of Architecture. (n.d.). *Twenty-five year award.* www.aia.org/awards/7141-twenty-five-year-award

Barrie, T. (1996). *Spiritual path, sacred place: Myth, ritual, and meaning in architecture.* Shambhala.

Congress for the New Urbanism. (n.d.). *About us.* www.cnu.org/who-we-are/movement

Crosbie, M. J. (2021). *Juhani Pallasmaa: Architecture is a verb.* https://commonedge.org/juhani-pallasmaa-architecture-is-a-verb/

de Botton, A. (2006). *The architecture of happiness.* Penguin Books.

Delos and Mayo Clinic. (n.d.). *Well Living Lab.* www.welllivinglab.com/

Forster, K. W. (1999). Why are some buildings more interesting than others? *Harvard Design Magazine, 7.* www.harvarddesignmagazine.org/issues/7/why-are-some-buildings-more-interesting-than-others

Goethe, J. W. von, Eckermann, J. P., & Fuller, M. (1839). *Conversations with Goethe in the last years of his life.* Hilliard, Gray and Company.

Goldhagen, S. (2020). *Welcome to your world: How the built environment shapes our lives.* Harper.

Heerwagen, J. H., Heubach, J. G., Montgomery, J., & Weimer, W. C. (1995). Environmental design, work, well being: Managing occupational stress through changes in the workplace environment. *AAOHN Journal, 43*(9), 458–468. https://doi. org/10.1177/216507999504300904

Howard, B., Moore, R., & Bush, J. (2016). *Zootopia.* Walt Disney Feature Animation.

Huang, T. T., Sorensen, D., Davis, S., Frerichs, L., Brittin, J., Celentano, J., et al. (2013). Healthy eating design guidelines for school architecture. *Centers for Disease Control and Prevention.* http://doi.org/10.5888/pcd10.120084. www.cdc. gov/pcd/issues/2013/pdf/12_0084.pdf

Hungerford, M. W. (1878). *Molly Bawn.* Smith, Ebber, & Co.

Hustwit, G. (2007). *Helvetica* [Documentary]. Swiss Dots Veer. shorturl.at/lrFWZ

Jacobs, J. (1992). *The death and life of great American cities.* Vintage Books.

Krier, L., Thadani, D. A., & Hetzel, P. J. (2009). *The architecture of community.* Island Press.

Murphy, M. (2016). *Architecture that's built to heal* [Video]. Ted Conferences. www. ted.com/talks/michael_murphy_architecture_that_s_built_to_heal?language=en

O'Donnell Wicklund Pigozzi and Peterson, Architects Inc. VS Furniture, & Bruce Mau Design (Eds.). (2010). *The third teacher: 79 ways you can use design to transform teaching & learning.* Abrams.

Ruskin, J. (1907). *The seven lamps of architecture.* B. Tauchnitz.

Saunders, W. (1999). From taste to judgment: Multiple criteria in the evaluation of architecture. *Harvard Design Magazine, 7.* www.harvarddesignmagazine.org/issues/7/ from-taste-to-judgment-multiple-criteria-in-the-evaluation-of-architecture

Schutz, A. (1962). *The problem of social reality: Collected papers I.* Martinus Nijhoff.

Shoup, J. R., & Hinrichs, T. W. (2020). *Literature and leadership: The role of the narrative in organizational sensemaking.* Routledge, Taylor, and Francis Group.

Tate, K., & Tate, D. (2019). *The alchemy of architecture: Memories and insight from Ken Tate.* Pearl Press.

Tuan, Y. (1977). *Space and place: The perspective of experience.* University of Minnesota Press.

Ulrich, R. P., Quan, X., Zimring, C. P., Joseph, A., & Choudhary, R. (2004). The role of the physical environment in the hospital of the 21st century: A once-in-a-lifetime opportunity. *The Center for Health Design.* www.healthdesign.org/knowledge- repository/role-physical-environment-hospital-21st-century-once-lifetime-opportunity

Um, S., & Buzzard, J. (2013). *Why cities matter: To God, the culture, and the church.* Crossway.

University of Notre Dame [UND]. (n.d.). *Throughout the years the tunnel in Notre Dame Stadium has become a special day.* https://und.com/throughout-the-years- the-tunnel-in-notre-dame-stadium-has-become-a-special-place/

Vitruvius. (1960). *The Ten books on architecture* (M. H. Morgan, Trans.). Dover Publications (Original work published 1914).

Weiner, E. (2012). Where heaven and earth come closer. *The New York Times.* www. nytimes.com/2012/03/11/travel/thin-places-where-we-are-jolted-out-of-old- ways-of-seeing-the-world.html

We Work. (n.d.). *Ideas.* www.wework.com/ideas

Yeazell, R. (2009). *Art of the everyday: Dutch painting and the realist novel.* Princeton University Press.

4 Critical Components of Architecture

Building Elements and Design Principles

Introduction

Architecture is more than defined space. We established that architecture is the art and science of creating habitable buildings and that it is so much more than that. We understand that architecture shelters us, but more than that it speaks to us. We know that architecture can be beautiful, but more than that, it communicates to us and shapes our view of the world and of ourselves. We aspire to make places that accomplish these things well. We want our built environments to be, in a word, good.

We know that buildings can move beyond minimal functional baselines to become meaningful places, enabling desired connections, engendering desired culture, and communicating desired values. Architecture can be great when designed based on sound principles and can be purposeful and uplifting to the lives of those who experience it. There are many beautiful examples of architecture rising to this level of meaning in the houses of worship, centers of government, museums, libraries, schools, monuments, and other public and private architecture all around us.

Unfortunately, we also know from our lived experiences that sometimes our built environment falls short. To create buildings which are good and avoid adding to this shortfall, we must identify those requirements that are essential to a place moving from solely functional or utilitarian to meaningful, from firmness to delight. Likewise, from a leadership perspective, we must identify how the physical context, the built environment, can be employed to successfully contribute to organizational identity, vision, mission, and goals.

This rise begins with an understanding of the goals and associated identifiable elements of good architecture. William Saunders (1999), in *From Taste to Judgment*, said:

> The designed environment should achieve art; create beauty; provide satisfying visceral experiences through scale, proportion, balance,

DOI: 10.4324/9781003166788-4

rhythm, texture, color, variation, pattern; harmonize function with image and symbolism; be original; blend unobtrusively with its surrounding environment; respond to the character of its region and climate; support and exemplify social/political goals and moral behavior; express the ideals of its community/society; cause no harm to the earth's ecosystem; be well crafted; realize the client's wants (not the architect's idea of what the client should want); realize the architect's goals; be durable; provide bodily and psychic comfort; achieve its ends economically; achieve good economic returns on investment; influence people to visit and return; contribute to high work productivity. One could, of course, go on.

(p. 132)

That is quite a long list of goals, and according to Saunders, still not comprehensive. Saunders (1999) went on to point out that some of these listed goals even contradict others. To enable one to grasp this effectively, we propose boiling all of this down to three Critical Components of Architecture: Building Elements, Design Principles, and Use Strategies. While each component serves a distinct and specific purpose, all three must be present and working together to achieve the kind of physical environments that can be useful to leaders and translate into leadership strategies. It is helpful to understand them uniquely.

Sadly, and perhaps too often, buildings are viewed as containers, somewhat disconnected from the real work that is done within. This is reflected, for example, in a leader saying, "we know exactly what we want to do and how we want to do it; now we just need a place in which to do it." In the church example from Chapter 1, much thought was given to the what and how of church operations such as worship services, preaching, singing, giving, childcare, etc. However, how the physical space would facilitate and support these activities was still ill-considered. The physical space design, which was the single element that cost the most money, took the most time, and would be the hardest to change later, was not thought about in the same way. This lack of attention to design ultimately dictated the church's strategy and capacity to meet its vision and goals. This absence of deliberate consideration will often result in organizations having to force their operations into spaces that were never designed to accommodate them, resulting in a need to adjust strategies to fit the space. Paying attention to building design is a strategic decision for leaders. The purpose of this chapter is to describe the meaning and importance of the first two of the Critical Components of Architecture: Building Elements and Design Principles. The third Critical Component, Use Strategies, will be discussed in the next chapter.

Critical Components of Architecture

Considering what we have discussed thus far, we propose a dialogical, reciprocal understanding of the three Critical Components of Architecture (Figure 4.1), Building Elements (which determine occupation), Design Principles (which determine experience), and Use Strategies (which determine flourishing). These three components are useful and applicable for leaders who want to create built environments that effectively reinforce their organization's vision, goals, and collective aspirations.

Building Elements are the basic building blocks of any structure or space. In all the examples we have explored within this book, Building Elements are those components that separate the inside from the outside, provide shelter, make the structure a habitable building, and indicate how the building will be used (e.g., an office building, a church, a government building, etc.). Design Principles are the generative design ideas common to great architecture that raise the level of architecture above that of those basic components. When chosen and applied well, design principles can elevate the building to a position of importance and meaning in a community. Use Strategies represent how one thinks about a constructed space's usage and programming schema, such as ensuring a proper, useable space to support values surrounding collaboration and communication within a space. An essential aspect of choosing Design Principles and designing Use Strategies to complement Building Elements is deciding not only how a space will be used, but also what values and ethos you want to communicate.

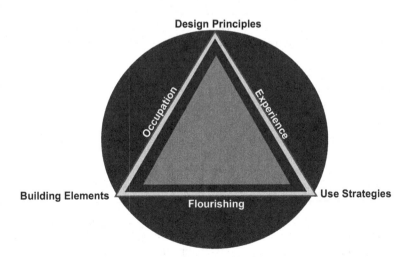

Figure 4.1 Critical Components of Architecture. Figure by Mark A. Roberson and Alicia Crumpton.

The three Critical Components of Architecture are dialogical in that for a place to be ultimately successful, no one component exists in isolation from the others. To understand how to arrange the basic Building Elements and how to design around the most importantly applicable Design Principles, one must first understand how and by whom the building will be used and for what it is intended. For a building to be useful as intended, one must understand the needed Building Elements and the most applicable Design Principles. An understanding of Design Principles must be present to understand how to successfully conncct Building Elements to Use Strategies and raise the building to the level of meaning and impact. Building Elements and universal Design Principles are discussed together in this chapter. The application of specific Design Principles is discussed in Chapter 5 and Use Strategies will be discussed separately in Chapter 6.

Building Elements

Recalling the church story with which Chapter 1 began, the building in question had all the requisite Building Elements to function at a basic level, to keep occupants dry and conditioned, to be accessible to the public, and to be identifiable as a church. The first of the two main things that John Ruskin (as cited in de Botton, 2006) said we wanted from our buildings is for them to shelter us, and the church met that requirement. This need for basic shelter seems obvious and was doubtless the original purpose that drove humans to build. It is the very foundation of what the built environment means and the purpose it serves. Building Elements are the physical attributes that form the buildings and spaces that shelter us. These elements are what define the limits of a building and establish its existence in the world, giving the building firmness.

Building Elements are those factors that contribute to a building meeting minimum standards for human use and occupation. Building elements include foundations, walls, floors, roofs, ceilings, doors, windows, structural systems, and most typically, building systems, including electrical, plumbing, heating, ventilation, and air conditioning (HVAC), accessible routes and elements, vertical conveyance, insulation, waterproofing, etc. Some combination of these elements will be found in every building, structure, and space, from tepees, huts, and lean-tos to the most technically advanced structures in the world. These elements are necessary for buildings to achieve compliance with building and safety codes and be permitted and certified for occupancy. These are also the most obvious and basic elements of a building, and their application is often self-explanatory. However, Building Elements are essential to comprehend and appreciate. Everyone understands that a building needs to shelter humans from the weather and be structurally sound, and typically include such necessary

Figure 4.2 The preserved remains of Catalhoyuk, Konya, Turkey. From: Northern Imagery, shutterstock.com.

features as walls, doors, stairs, lights, and toilets. Without these basic elements, a building is not possible at all.

Looking back through the history of built form, we see that ancient structures such as Catalhoyuk (Figure 4.2), the Tower of Jericho, and Newgrange are buildings that contain a number of these same Building Elements, even without the requirement of modern building codes.

We've come a long way with plumbing, lighting, HVAC, and technology since those buildings were constructed. Still, we find that these ancient structures contained cleared floors, walls, roof structures, interior rooms, passageways, windows, and even staircases for vertical conveyance. If you go to work in a typical shipping warehouse today, there may not be much attention paid to scale and proportion. Still, the structure will contain all those same components as those ancient examples. The typical tilt-up concrete warehouse structure will stand up, it will keep the rain out, the lights will turn on, the toilets will flush, and there will be sufficient ventilation and exiting.

If you were to visit Apple Park, Apple's headquarters in Cupertino, California (Figure 4.3), you would find one of the most technologically advanced buildings in the world, powered by 100% renewable energy, and the largest LEED Platinum certified office building in North America (Foster & Partners, n.d.). Yet this amazing structure is still made with and defined by these same basic Building Elements.

Figure 4.3 Aerial view of the Apple Park campus, Cupertino, CA. From SnapASkyline, shutterstock.com.

Design Principles

Design Principles are different from Building Elements, in that they are not necessary for buildings to be built, to stand, or to be useful, as described in the discussion of delight. A cursory look will reveal many examples of buildings standing in the world and functioning to at least some extent, without having had any Design Principles applied to their design at all. Design Principles, according to principles.design (n.d.), are "a set of considerations that form the basis of any good product." Within architecture, Design Principles are not the basis of the building's existence but contribute significantly to the building being declared good. The writers at principles.design (n.d.) go on to say that "A few simple principles . . . will guide your team towards making appropriate decisions." Once again, Design Principles are not just guides to making decisions but guides to informing better decision making. A Google search will result in articles outlining the 12 basic principles of design, or the 8 basic principles, or the 7, or the 6, or the 5, or the 3. While it seems that there is no consensus on the exact number of basic Design Principles, there is a consensus understanding that Design Principles are what make a design good or appropriate.

The intentional employment of such principles in architecture raises the design of buildings above the basic level of existence and functionality that Building Elements provide, in a way that is truly unique to architecture. If a poster, logo, work of art, or a film is not good, they have typically not achieved any minimum level of usability. Their ability to connect and speak to an audience is their basic purpose, and without that ability, they have failed. Architecture can exist without considering such principles and still fulfill its basic purpose and utility, as exemplified by most any local strip-mall or warehouse. This is the uniqueness that habitability provides. However, our aim here is to understand what gives buildings meaning and even virtue. de Botton (2006) described virtuous buildings as those having order, balance, elegance, coherence, and self-knowledge, or in summary, applied Design Principles.

The intentional application and consideration of Design Principles in the conception and design of a building is what gives that building the power to affect the lives of those who experience it in many positive ways. The absence of well-considered Design Principles results in buildings that may not have such positive effects, or worse yet, produce adverse or ill effects. Moreover, it is the understanding of both Design Principles and Use Strategies that will allow leaders to shape the Building Elements contributive to their physical environments into meaningful and significant places that are powerful facilitators of organizational identity, mission, purpose, and culture.

There are various lists of Design Principles in various places from various authors of varying levels of renown and seriousness that feature some combination of principles such as balance, rhythm, proportion, scale, movement, unity, contrast, hierarchy, context, transformation, emphasis, alignment, focal point, pattern, symmetry, axis, and others. Some of these principles appear on virtually every list and have thus appeared for centuries. In fact, several of these go back to the same 2,000-year-old Vitruvian text introduced earlier. In his *Ten Books of Architecture*, Vitruvius (1960) described several Design Principles incorporated as the visual and physical application of the architectural trinity of firmness, utility, and delight. These ancient Vitruvian principles will be discussed, along with a few others that have similarly stood the test of time. The explanation of these principles will be supplemented with examples illustrative of each so that you can better grasp each Design Principle and what it looks like in application.

There are two large categories of Design Principles that contribute to a building's meaning and virtue. The first category are principles that are foundational, in that these are wide in effect and universally identifiable across all great architecture. The second category are Design Principles specifically applicable to individual situations. Understanding the effects of both types of Design Principles will then allow leaders to intentionally employ selections or combinations of them to communicate specific messages unique to their organizational identity, mission, and values.

We begin this discussion of Design Principles by laying out and illuminating those foundational Principles which are possessed across the spectrum of great architecture. It is these three overarching Principles of context, story, and fittedness to which all the others contribute and to which architecture aspires. We will discuss these supporting, specifically applicable Principles in the following chapter. But first, we will understand how creating architecture that is rooted in its context, successfully tells an intended story, and is, in the end, fitted and proper for its place and use, should be the goal of every architect and every leader.

In the cases that follow, examples are included of varying scale and scope. These illustrate that whether one is considering a new corporate headquarters on the scale of Apple Park, or simply considering a novel approach to office furniture such as at SEI (West & Wind, 2007), a clear understanding and intentional employment of Design Principles will profoundly impact an organization's physical environment, and as a result, the shaping and communication of organizational identity, mission, and values.

Foundational Design Principles: Context, Story, and Fittedness

All great stories have a beginning, middle, and end. Classical architectural elements feature a base, shaft, capital, or a beginning, middle, and end similarly. In music, three-part harmonies are made up of, three parts: low, middle, and high. Humans are thought to possess body, mind, and spirit. So, it is with Design Principles. All the significant, meaningful, and enduring architecture that has marked the course of human civilization began with the idea of context, progressed through the structure of story, and achieved in the end what Vitruvius (1960) called propriety or fittedness. This cycle begins with the idea that the meaningful and lasting architecture of the world is rooted in its Context.

Context

Architecture is always situated in a specific time and place. Architecture that is considered great is rooted in and built on a foundational understanding of, and reaction to, that context, including such factors as people, history, physical environment, culture, politics, climate, economy, and ecology. All these factors should influence architectural design in a way that grounds the design in shared human experiences such that those who live within a context will know, feel, and connect to the design. Context refers to the full historical situatedness of a place.

Response to context resonates with us because there are many personal contextual experiences that establish the armature upon which our lives are constructed. The context of our lives derives from good moments and bad, from amazement and discouragement – moments that leave a lasting impression on our soul. Often, the amazing moments occur when we experience creative beauty – breathtaking natural elements, great works of art, music, theatrical performances, or films. We are then reminded of the context where this happened. For example, imagine you hear a song that's meaningful to a significant other and you, a song that transports you back to that specific and memorable time, place, or person. So too it is with architecture. Vital to our capacity to remember and recall is an association with place and the built environment. German Philosopher Martin Heidegger (1971) said that our very existence is a condition of dwelling. Thus, like a body on a skeleton, our lives are built on the armature of the lived and understood context of our lives.

Great architecture is that which is similarly built on the armature of its context, and then it becomes part of that context, which pushes us forward to what's next – to new understandings of the world. Timeless architecture is that which begins its existence completely founded in and connected to its own time and context. This foundation of context gives architecture (and other works) authenticity. The idea of fittedness is related to this sense of a building's authenticity. Most people appreciate such authenticity and can sense when something is fake. We more highly value an antique than we do an exact reproduction. Visiting the Statue of Liberty in New York Harbor is a more highly valued experience than visiting the replica at New York, New York Casino in Las Vegas or one of the many other replicas around the world. This is because the original represents a certain time, place, and moment in history and has a story of how it came to be and how it survived the ensuing years to be with us today that a replica can never match. Buildings must have meaningful authenticity through their basis in their context, to have real, lasting impact and to be considered great.

For most of the history of our built environment, the state of building technology and materials meant that being contextual was really the only option available. For example, the Ziggurat of Ur, built in the 21st century BC, was made of mud bricks from the surrounding materials and sealed together with more local mud to resist climactic conditions. The design of the building then responded to this construction technique. More recent examples, such as 100-year-old farmhouses in central Texas, show similar traits as they were typically built from locally quarried stone, had porches to keep the sun from hitting the exterior walls, metal roofs to reflect solar heat, and typically cross or central ventilation to move hot air through and out. These buildings were naturally contextual in many ways. However, advancements in building materials and technology allowed the creation of new styles that ignore context and are nonauthentic revivals of past styles, giving designers the ability to create French Chateaus with Italian marble kitchens and Vermont slate roofs, which have no connection to their place or situation.

When one examines the great architecture of the world, virtually none of it is such an inauthentic copy of something else or of a style that is foreign to its location and time. It is all derived from its context. The church example described in Chapter 1 could have benefitted from additional contextual analysis such as understanding:

1. The physical location and neighborhood of the site, including the demographics of those who currently lived or were moving there.
2. The forms, shapes, and visual designs of other buildings in the neighborhood, including symbols and images important to those they were trying to reach.
3. The ethnic and cultural makeup of the neighborhood, including cultural traditions, community practices, etc.
4. The needs of the local community and people within it.

Starting with a contextual analysis is a useful and helpful way to gather information and learn about the context of a proposed building. Four amazing examples of projects that took this idea of context very seriously are explored: the Jean-Marie Tjibaou Cultural Center, the Kaufmann House, Thorncrown Chapel, and the Hill Country Jackel. These examples are beautiful architectural solutions of varying scale and purpose that emerged completely from their contexts.

The Jean-Marie Tjibaou Cultural Center in New Caledonia (Figure 4.4), designed by architect Renzo Piano and finished in 1991, is a beautiful example of this idea of a design which begins with and results from its unique context.

This project was inspired by and designed to celebrate the history, culture, beliefs, and environment of the indigenous Kanak people of New Caledonia. A series of huts were designed to echo a local Kanak village and the individual buildings are curved in shape to reference traditional Kanak construction. Wood rib and slat exterior walls echo the traditional woven vegetable fiber walls of Kanak huts. The semi-circular layout of the buildings creates a traditional village communal space with all the buildings connected by footpaths cutting through lush native vegetation, as would be the huts in a traditional village.

Figure 4.4 Close up view of the construction details of the Jean-Marie Tjibaou Cultural Center in New Caledonia. From EQRoy, shutterstock.com.

These buildings, as much as they echo the Kanak culture and are products of their cultural context, are not copies of Kanak architecture from another time. Instead, they are reflections of their own time using available materials and technology, including highly efficient, passive ventilation systems that harness the monsoon winds; building components of glass, aluminum, and steel; and modern lighting systems. According to designer Renzo Piano Building Workshop (n.d.), the Center "pays homage to Kanak culture and draws on local building traditions and expertise by intertwining the ancient and the modern." Furthermore, in discussing the design process, Renzo Piano Building Workshop (n.d.) noted,

> An understanding of the development of Kanak culture was a vital part of this project – becoming familiar with Kanak history, environment and beliefs made it possible to design a building that would fit within this context . . . Taking inspiration from the Kanak people's deep ties with nature, the project sought to meet two main objectives: one was to represent the Kanak's talent for building, and the other was the use of modern materials such as glass, aluminum, steel and

modern light technologies along with the more traditional wood and stone.

The result is a collection of beautiful, modern buildings widely recognized as great architecture, which are completely a product of their location, culture, climate, history, politics, and time that could not have existed anywhere else in the world.

For iconic American architect Frank Lloyd Wright, responding to the natural setting of a building and to the people who would inhabit it were important contextual elements that inspired his designs. The Kaufmann House at Bear Run, Pennsylvania (Figure 4.5), better known as Fallingwater, is an incredible example of this idea from 1939.

Wright recognized the power and beauty of the dominant horizontal stone ledges that Bear Run River has worn through as it pursued its path. He also appreciated the immense pleasure that his clients derived from experiencing the waterfalls of Bear Run. To respond to this physical and experiential context, Wright designed a house made up of horizontal plates that appear to have been cut through, and located it directly over the waterfall, providing the house's inhabitants the most direct possible connection to the water. This contextual response exists so uniquely as a product of its place and

Figure 4.5 The Kaufmann House at Bear Run, PA, better known as Fallingwater, a perfect merging of architecture and context. From: Ventiviews, unsplash.com.

time that Fallingwater was declared as the "best all-time work of American architecture" by the American Institute of Architecture (franklloydwright. org, n.d.).

At Thorncrown Chapel in Eureka Springs, Arkansas (Figure 4.6) (1980), a past winner of the AIA Twenty-five Year Award, architect E. Fay Jones was inspired by the stunning landscape, as well as "shapes and materials, methods of building character, and associative cultural and remembered image evocations" (Heyer, 1993, pp. 102–103). This building is so much a part of its landscape and region that it seemingly could not exist in the same way in any other place or time. Thorncrown's vertical wooden structure and glass walls make the building almost disappear into the surrounding forest. There is almost no separation between being inside the building and being outside in the forest.

Beyond this, the building form and shape is also symbolically reminiscent of covered bridges which are popular and plentiful in the area. Heyer (1993) said of this symbolism, "the image of shelter on the road of life is in keeping with the ecclesiastical understanding of nature" (pp. 102–103).

These three examples represent world-class architectural masterworks. They were presented to give easily identifiable visual examples illustrative of the foundational principle of Context. For a much smaller scale but still highly successful example, we look to Pipe Creek, Texas.

Figure 4.6 The Thorncrown Chapel, blending into the woods of Eureka Springs, AR. From Rachael Martin, shutterstock.com.

Figure 4.7 Hill Country Jackal, Pipe Creek, TX, by Lake Flato Architects. Courtesy of © Leigh Christian Photography.

Lake Flato Architects has earned a reputation for designing buildings that seamlessly fit the context of the Central Texas Hill Country around San Antonio and Austin. The Hill Country Jackal (Figure 4.7), located on a rock ledge overlooking a creek northwest of San Antonio, is a very small-scale yet beautiful example of this principle.

This 1997 ranch house is a modern, timely interpretation of the traditional Hill Country ranch house going back almost two centuries. The house is constructed of local limestone walls, cedar structure, screening, and a simple metal shed roof, fashioned as a very traditional lean-to structure. This house is designed to take advantage of the prevailing breezes and the view to the creek, to block out the chilly winter winds, to provide ample shade and reflect the summer heat, and to be tied unquestionably to its place through form and material.

This deep understanding of the context with which you start to design, things like time, place, people, weather, economy, history, political climate, etc. – all the interrelated conditions in which something exists, is the foundational principle from which great architecture springs. And an appreciation of and appropriate response to the context is the basis of architecture becoming a meaningful and memorable place.

Story

Storytelling has been with us since the beginning of civilization. Everything from the origins of human understanding of the universe and of God to our current discussion of big data is communicated through story. Visual storytelling, according to American filmmaker Frank Darabont (as cited in Wallace, 2007) "has been around since cavemen were drawing on the walls." Furthermore,

> Throughout time, people have used visual devices to capture stories. Visual storytelling displays a history of the past, an identity for the present, and a story for the future to compare and appreciate. Architecture is an ever-present form of visual storytelling. The built environment can capture the history of a place and tell that story through space. In this way, architecture forms a visual, spatial link between the past, present, and future, becoming a point in the timeline of a place and culture.
>
> (Wallace, 2007)

Storytelling and buildings orient our lives. In stories, we imagine others navigating the world, but in buildings, we get to live out the story as we navigate the experience personally. Unfortunately, those leading building projects sometimes don't overtly consider or perceive the built environment as having a role in telling an organization's story. This lack of consideration contributes to architecture that lacks depth and genuine connection to context. Buildings lacking this storytelling within the design communicate nothing of a place's history or culture, but instead present a dissonant, false, or even oppositional story based purely on a style appropriated from another place, time, and meaning. For example, a church desires to appeal to a millennial audience but builds a building designed to look like a pre-WWII structure. A restaurant describing its food as homestyle comfort food has an interior that is stark white, cool blue, and minimal. These sorts of disconnects between values and design are experienced as such by those who engage with architecture, decreasing the likelihood that the building will be perceived as desired. This idea of understanding the story your physical place will tell is essential to that place accurately communicating your organizational values and identity.

Architecture can build story based on the foundation of its context, addressing the present while inspiring consideration for the future. There are many examples of how this can work. Sometimes the program of a building, its physical shape, its specific location, or a combination of all of these, reflects and continues to express the existing and ongoing story of a place, such as the Church of the Holy Sepulchre in Jerusalem. The church, originally erected by Constantine in the 4th century AD, sits on the traditional site of Jesus' death and burial. This church then captures the essence of its historical context, preserving, expressing and becoming a part of the story of that place. Then there are times when the architecture's very purpose is to tell a story that it wholly creates and nurtures, such as Disneyland Park. Disneyland designer and artist John Hench (2009) observed, "Story is the essential organizing principle behind the design of the Disney theme parks. Imagineers interpret and create narratives for guests to experience in real space and time" (p. 67).

Other times, when the story communicated by the building doesn't come from its context, and is not intentionally escapist fantasy, there can be unintended yet very real consequences. For example, noted American architect Michael Graves' Portland Building, finished in 1982, is a postmodern icon that is the embodiment of a false story based on the whimsical imagination of the architect and having no relation to the context of the place or the purpose of the building.

As a result of this design approach, the Portland Building, according to the documentary *Beyond Utopia: Changing Attitudes in American Architecture*

Figure 4.8 Looking up at the controversial Portland Building, Portland, OR. From: EQRoy, shutterstock.com.

(Blackwood, 2014), is said to have dire effects on the physical and mental health of its occupants, even to the point of causing depression.

A building derived from its context continues to be meaningful, holding an important position over time, based on the story it tells and the stories that become attached to it over the course of its existence. Such a building will then become part of the story of the place, creating a new layer to the story and a new future story to tell.

Few buildings in the world tell their intended story as well and as thoroughly as The Jewish Museum Berlin (Figure 4.9), which opened in 2001.

The museum is a building designed specifically to tell the story of the Jewish people in Berlin, Germany, and to do so without the need for any words or external interpretation. This is a tall order for such a static and silent thing as a building to accomplish. Still, American architect Daniel Libeskind was able to design a building that does just that in a powerful, moving way. The intended story is very carefully and thoughtfully advanced through the interior plan, circulation and materials, the exterior materials, colors, and openings, and even the landscape design, including the specific plants chosen.

By creating a distorted and seemingly torn Star of David, this disfigured symbol of the Jewish faith became the floorplan of the building. Spatially,

Figure 4.9 The exterior materials and windows of the Jewish Museum Berlin evoke cut and scarred skin. Berlin, Germany. From PictureNet/Corbis via Getty Images.

this museum is connected via a zig-zagging dark passage to an older Jewish Museum such that this connection "links the old and new buildings, the city's history with Jewish history" (Schneider & Libeskind, 1999, p. 48). Six vertical shafts or voids pierce this dark, stark passage. These voids "evoke the gap that evolved in German and European culture and history by the destruction of Jewish lives on every floor of the museum. The museum is pervaded by this absence" (Schneider & Libeskind, 1999, p. 53).

The last of the voids that visitors reach is called the Holocaust Tower and is a "closed, bare, empty, and unheated space, its darkness penetrated only by a sharp beam from its single window, exerts an extremely compelling effect on anyone who experiences it" (Schneider & Libeskind, 1999, p. 51). There is a hallway from the underground passageway that leads to the sunken Garden of Exile, and this is the only way to access the outside world from below ground, "evoking the idea of exile as the only way to freedom" (Schneider & Libeskind, 1999, p. 50). The Garden of Exile provides visitors with a tight, uncomfortable space with columns oriented to the sloping pavement, causing a feeling of disorientation. The landscape continues telling the story in the Locust Grove, which "represents a tiny piece of untamed wilderness, sprung up from the soil of destruction, the rubble of the war-torn city, and is surrounded by artfully arranged greenery" (Schneider & Libeskind, 1999). Roses were also used, as they were the only plant permitted in the ancient city of Jerusalem. All in all, this building is a powerful story-telling device that tells exactly the story that was intended by leveraging every possible design decision. Those who come to this place and experience this story then add their own reactions and memories to the layering of meaning accomplished here.

The renovation of the historic Tower Theater in downtown Los Angeles (Figure 4.10) was an effort by Apple to tell their own story as an extension of the story of Los Angeles and the region as the dominant hub of creativity in the world.

Describing the importance of Apple Tower, Dierdre O'Brien (2021), Apple's senior vice president of Retail + People, said in an Apple news release: "At every corner, Los Angeles bursts with creativity across the arts, music, and entertainment, and we are thrilled to build on our relationship with this special city." Apple Tower Theatre honors the rich history and legacy of this entertainment capital.

Los Angeles is the original home of talking pictures, and Apple sees its products as the newest generation of that lineage. The 1927 Tower Theater was also the first theater in Los Angeles wired for film with sound, a major technological advancement in film production and exhibition, and Apple is continuing that story with their own technologically advanced products offered in this same space. The floor area of the former auditorium will continue to be used in the spirit of its original purpose. Today at Apple Creative

Figure 4.10 Main interior space of the Apple Tower Store, Los Angeles, CA. From: Ringo Chiu, shutterstock.com.

Studios LA will offer free, daily sessions on creativity to provide inspiration and teach practical skills.

John Hench (2009) said of Disneyland Park (Figure 4.11), "Form begins with story, and renders each situation within the story in primarily visual terms" (p. 5). Disneyland Park, which opened in 1955 in Anaheim, California, is an exercise in using the built environment to create a story that didn't exist before.

The entire Disney empire is built on storytelling. Disneyland Park is the original effort at a physical manifestation of those stories, with the express intent of using story to escape reality and create an immersive experience of the "happiest place on earth." Hench (2009) observed:

> As designers, we Imagineers create spaces – guided experiences that take place in carefully structured environments, allowing our guests to see, hear, even smell, touch and taste in new ways . . . We give power to the guests' imagination, to transcend their everyday routine.
>
> (p. 2)

In pursuit of this effort to make a physical place that transcended the everyday routine, the entire planning of the park was envisioned as relating to the story of going to a movie and/or watching TV, which had been Disney's forte up to the advent of Disneyland. Urban planner and author

Figure 4.11 Cinderella's Castle, Disneyland Park, Anaheim, CA. Photo by Mark A. Roberson.

Sam Gennawey (2013) stated: "The use of filmmaking techniques in the design of Disneyland would become one of the park's signature elements" (p. 21). When one walks into the park, they are greeted by a marquee announcing that you have arrived at Disneyland, acting as a symbolic lobby. One then passes under the railroad to the right or left and through a tunnel with movie posters on the walls, as though you are passing into the darkened space of a theater. As you enter the tunnel, you pass under a sign (Figure 4.12) that reads, "Here you leave today and enter the world of yesterday, tomorrow, and fantasy," which is the exact intent of the architecture.

One then emerges onto Main Street USA, and the show begins as you proceed toward Cinderella's Castle. There is a circular plaza around the castle that acts almost like a TV remote control, in that from here, you can choose which experience you want to enter, or which show you want to watch – Tomorrowland, Adventureland, Fantasyland, etc. The rides, attractions, and themes of each land are then based around Disney movies and properties, immersing one into familiar, fantastic stories and promoting those stories to the buying public. And of course, every ride or

Figure 4.12 Welcome sign over entry tunnel leading to Main St., Disneyland Park, Anaheim, CA. Photo courtesy of Jeannette Cona-Larock.

experience ends in a giftshop (or so it seems) so that you can leave each land with a reminder of the experience. But just like most people didn't watch the movie Titanic because they wondered if the boat would sink at the end, but for the story of how it got there, you care about the giftshop only because you were led through a story that gives you a reason to want to remember it.

This is all achievable because literally everything you see, hear, touch, taste, and even smell has been intentionally designed to create that story. There are more than 100 disciplines represented in Disney's Imagineering wing, from architects to landscape architects to interior designers to engineers, writers, model makers, filmmakers, sociologists, robotics experts, and many more. This represents perhaps the most holistic effort to build story that exists in the world physically. As Hench (2009) explained, "In designing Disneyland, we thought of the park as if it were a three-dimensional film. We wanted everything that the guests experience, not only the shows and rides, to be an entertaining part of the story" (p. 23).

Storytelling through architecture is powerful and effective in communicating culture and purpose for those who are part of and those who experience and interact with an organization. Architecture that is based on its context and tells a meaningful story, becomes architecture that is fitted to its place and purpose.

Fittedness

The principle that comes last on Vitruvius' (1960) original list of Design Principles is also one that we present as the resultant universal characteristic of great architecture, that of fittedness. This idea of fittedness is a summarizing principle that proposes the idea that great architecture must be founded on its context, tell the story of its place, inspire a better future, and be a work substantially based on the other design principles we will discuss, to be just the exact piece of architecture in just the right place at just the right time. It fits, it is proper, and we know it to be so. A building that is just so will continue to have meaning beyond itself through the test of time. Vitruvius (1960) stated, "Propriety is that perfection of style which comes when a work is authoritatively constructed on approved principles. It arises from prescription, from usage, or from nature." Vitruvius suggested there must be some basis to and reason for design decisions made in the formulation of a building. Otherwise, the design will not be balanced, symmetrical, rhythmic, proportional, or ordered, and it will not result in a building that is a proper fit for the situation. Understanding and employing these ideas of context and story and the sound principles of design derived from accepted norms, historical precedent, or nature is essential to the long-lasting and meaningful success of the design of a building. In other words, if you start with an understanding of context, then tell an intentional, meaningful story, the result will be a building that exhibits fittedness over time.

The Kaufmann House at Bear Run, Pennsylvania, or Fallingwater, (Figure 4.5) is not just a great example of a design emerging from its context. It is also an example of what happens when a design that tells a story of a place and a people becomes a building that one cannot imagine being anything or anywhere else. It is the perfect, proper, fitted solution for that waterfall on that river for that purpose, for as long as it stands. That's why, 80 years after it was built, it is still considered a masterpiece of American architecture. One can't imagine Paris without the Eiffel Tower (Figure 3.1) sitting exactly where it is, looking exactly as it does. It is a building that started with the physical context of both its exact location within Paris and the technological, political, and economic context of the industrial revolution. Even though it was not widely understood or embraced when built, it was designed to express these stories very well and has stood the test of time to become one of the most proper and fitted buildings in the world.

The same can be said for the Sydney Opera House (Figure 3.10), St Peter's Basilica in Rome (Figure 4.19), the Robie House in Chicago, and many more examples of what is considered great architecture. Even Disneyland Park (Figure 4.11), which sprang from the mind of Walt Disney as a response to the context of himself, his company and entertainment venues of his day, and was completely invented to tell a story of Disney's creation, is, more than 60 years later, the perfectly proper and fitted solution for its place and purpose.

So, we understand the beginning, middle, and end of great architecture – that it must emerge from its context and tell an intentional story, resulting in a building that is proper and fitted. Interestingly, these same big-picture ideas exist in the leading of an organization. The leadership strategy employed will be most proper and fitted if it is derived from the organizational context and tells an authentic story of the organization, which we've seen play out in successful companies like Apple, Tom's Shoes, Burt's Bees, and many others.

Chapter Summary

When Building Elements and Design Principles are understood and employed intentionally, each contributes to people's sense of community, productivity, creativity, innovation, health, and overall commitment. Ultimately, the goal is to create architecture that echoes our human values:

> You shouldn't make people feel less . . . space should enhance them . . . it should be uplifting, instructive, and positive. . . . The best architecture provides for the physical, emotional, and intellectual needs of people who experience it.
>
> (Frank Gehry as cited in Cruikshank & Malcolm, 1994, pp. 3, 5)

We next explore the category of specifically applied Design Principles more deeply, and how those Principles accomplish distinct end effects, relative to an organization's specific situation and goals.

References

Blackwood, M. (2014). *Beyond Utopia: Changing attitudes in American architecture* [Documentary]. Michael Blackwood Productions.

Cruikshank, J. L., & Malcolm, C. (1994). *Herman Miller, Inc.: Buildings and beliefs.* The American Institute of Architects Press.

de Botton, A. (2006). *The architecture of happiness.* Penguin Books.

Foster and Partners. (n.d.). *Apple park.* www.fosterandpartners.com/projects/apple-park/

Franklloydwright.org. (n.d.). *Fallingwater.* https://franklloydwright.org/site/fallingwater/

Gennawey, S. (2013). *Disneyland story: The Unofficial guide to the evolution of Walt Disney's dream.* Unofficial Guides.

Heidegger, M. (1971). Building dwelling thinking. In M. Heidegger (Ed.), *Poetry, language, thought* (pp. 145–161, Translation and introduction: Albert Hofstadter). Harper & Row.

Hench, J. (2009). *Designing Disney: Imagineering and the art of the show (A Walt Disney Imagineering Book)*. Disney Editions.

Heyer, P. (1993). *American architecture: Ideas and ideologies in the late twentieth century*. Van Nostrand Reinhold.

O'Brien, D. (2021). *Apple tower theatre opens thursday in downtown Los Angeles*. www.apple.com/newsroom/2021/06/apple-tower-theatre-opens-thursday-in-downtown-los-angeles/

principles.design. (n.d.). *Design principles: An open source collection of design principles and methods*. https://principles.design/

Renzo Piano Building Workshop. (n.d.) *Jean-marie Tjibaou cultural center: 1991–1998 Noumea, New Caledonia*. www.rpbw.com/project/jean-marie-tjibaou-cultural-center

Saunders, W. (1999). From taste to judgment: Multiple criteria in the evaluation of architecture. *Harvard Design Magazine, 7*. www.harvarddesignmagazine.org/issues/7/from-taste-to-judgment-multiple-criteria-in-the-evaluation-of-architecture

Schneider, B., & Libeskind, D. (1999). *Daniel Libeskind: Jewish Museum Berlin*. Prestel.

Vitruvius. (1960). *The Ten books on architecture* (M. H. Morgan, Trans.). Dover Publications (Original work published 1914).

Wallace, C. (2007). Storytelling through architecture. *Chancellor's Honors Program Projects*. https://trace.tennessee.edu/utk_chanhonoproj/1129

West, A. P., & Wind, J. (2007). Putting the organization on wheels: Workplace design at SEI. *California Management Review, 49*(2), 138–153. http://doi.org/10.2307/41166387

5 Three Categories of Specific Design Principles

Introduction

The individual Design Principles discussed next are specific tools used that support, build on, and make the big-picture foundational Principles of the previous chapter come to successful fruition. Unlike those previously discussed Principles, not all these Principles will be seen in every great building. The context from which you begin and the unique story you want to tell will result in different but specific collections of applied Design Principles that can reinforce organizational vision and leadership in very specific ways. Understanding these and their applicability is essential to achieving a great built environment for your organization. The purpose of this chapter is to describe these specific Design Principles and group them into understandable, manageable categories. These categories contribute to: (Group A) the enjoyment and comfort of a viewer or user, such as order, rhythm, and proportion; (Group B) an understanding of a building's relative importance, such as balance, scale, and circulation; and (Group C) the preparation of the user to participate in things reflective, contemplative and inspiring, such as harmony, color and sensory engagement.

Group A: Order, Rhythm, and Proportion

The first set of these Design Principles considered have long been vital to the never-ending search for beauty in architecture. These principles are specifically intended to bring calm, peace, and comfort to the experiencer by providing conditions that humans expect, understand, and find comforting. We expect to find the discrete parts of things to exist in some regular order, in relative proportionality to each other. When there is a left, we expect a right. Nature tells us that these conditions are correct and even beautiful, and these principles, when incorporated into architecture, provide that same sense of rightness and even beauty. Buildings lacking these conditions

DOI: 10.4324/9781003166788-5

are typically not considered comfortable, right, or beautiful, sometimes to intended effect, but most often not so. If calm, peace, and beauty are intended goals in the physical environment, leaders should consider this group of principles that provide esthetic quality, comfort, reassurance, and enjoyment. In this section, we look specifically at the principles of order, rhythm, and proportion, illustrating the effects of these principles through examples of various types and sizes.

Order

The first of this set of principles is Order, one of the design principles identified 2,000 years ago in the writings of Vitruvius. Of Order, Vitruvius (1960) said, "Order gives due measure to the members of a work considered separately, and symmetrical agreement to the proportions of the whole." He continued, "By this I mean the selection of modules from the members of the work itself and, starting from these individual parts of members, constructing the whole work to correspond." What Vitruvius is saying is that the whole work must be a result of (correspond to) the individual parts. The parts can't be made to fit into a predetermined whole. He referred to it as, "The elegance of effect which is due to adjustments appropriate to the character of the work." Vitruvius recognizes the importance of not just making the whole the sum of the parts but of understanding the nature and strength of the individual parts to ensure they are all used in accordance with their purpose.

Two millennia later, these same ideas were being extolled concerning leadership by Jim Collins (2001) in *Good to Great* as getting the right people on the bus and then getting them into the right seats by recognizing their strengths and purpose. This was expressed by architect Louis Sullivan (1896) as "form follows function." All the parts of which a work of architecture is made, and the reason for which it is made, should determine the final form and expression. Those parts and functions should never be subservient to some predetermined formal or even stylistic idea but rather must be used according to their strength and purpose, in their proper place and time.

A great example of a building designed around this relationship of the parts to the whole and of using all the parts to create overall order is the Parthenon (Figure 5.1) in Athens, Greece.

In ancient Greece, the physical environment mirrored culture in many ways, including the pursuit of perfect Order in architecture. The Parthenon represents the culmination of a wholly committed pursuit of built order, consistent with the ancient Greek pursuit of continual development and refinement of their culture and society. The Parthenon is the centerpiece of a 5th century BC building project on the Acropolis in Athens and is considered the perfection of the classical Doric Order. Each part, the base and steps, the

Figure 5.1 Parthenon, Athens, Greece. From Christopher Chan/Moment via Getty Images.

columns, the frieze, the pediment, the relationship of the height, width, and length, and even the smallest details, are all designed very specifically and intentionally to create a cohesive and perfect whole. The resulting building makes it clear that order, and human's ability to construct order out of the natural world's disorder to provide the experience of comfort, enjoyment, and beauty, was the chief aim of this work of architecture.

The Salk Institute in La Jolla, California, finished in 1965 and a past winner of the AIA Twenty-five Year Award, is a modern interpretation of the ideas of the Parthenon. The Salk, by revered American architect Louis Kahn, consists of two rectangular buildings composed of repeated vertical elements surrounding an interior courtyard space. Those two buildings are arranged symmetrically around the courtyard, which has a linear water channel running down its central axis.

The regularity of the pieces, their size, shape, and spacing, and the simplicity of the material elements create an arrangement that is very ordered, symmetrical, clear, and understandable, which gives one a sense of fulfilled expectations, peace, comfort, and enjoyment. The feelings that the Order of this building and courtyard space generate have made it a popular location for weddings, commencement ceremonies, and even funerals.

The Jewish Museum in Berlin (Figure 4.9) discussed previously is an architecture of disorder, pointing out the power of Order as vividly as any orderly design ever could. This building intentionally employs disorder

Figure 5.2 Central courtyard and water channel of Salk Institute, La Jolla, California.
From: Adam Bignell, unsplash.com.

and unexpected arrangement to tell its story of pain and sorrow, with precariously tilted elements, tight passageways, sloping ground planes, harsh materials, and darkness. This disorder creates discomfort, distress, and a complete lack of enjoyment, and that is precisely the point. No one wants to get married or celebrated here because the feelings generated by this building are not ones that lead to looking back warmly and happily.

Rhythm

The next design principle that Vitruvius (1960) wrote about is Rhythm, "beauty and fitness in the adjustments of the members." The members, the ordered pieces that make up the whole, are to be arranged in such a way that relate well to each other. We have seen Rhythm as an element of Order, but more specifically, the pieces must be spaced out correctly, not bunched up or crowded, given the chance to exist with peace and comfort. Rhythm would suggest that there is a piece, a member, exactly where you would expect one to be and not where one shouldn't be, much like a beat in music. Day (2014) observed that "when we repeat things and the spaces between them, we start to make a rhythm . . . repetition is the basis of rhythm. It can bring an anchoring structure" (p. 27). Humans can notice instantly and respond to the rhythm within a space, to the comfort of things being as and where they should be, or to dissonance if something feels off. This means that the pieces fit the spaces thus created by their rhythmic placement, not being too large or too small for their space. The Order of the Parthenon and the Salk Institute works so well because of the rhythm and proportion of the parts. The physics of structure and the realities of pre-determined building material units make Rhythm, by default, one of the more commonly exercised of these Design Principles. That is why we find this principle present in many great buildings across the world throughout history, including our examples here.

The Zentrum Paul Klee (Figure 5.3) in Bern, Switzerland, is another brilliant building that displays many of the principles discussed, and one particularly strong principle on display here is that of Rhythm, which gives the building its unique character. This building, designed by Renzo Piano Building Workshop and completed in 2005, begins with its context in many ways. It has a rolling, wave-like form inspired by the gentle rolling hills that surround it.

The repeated lines of the roof were inspired by the vast cultivated fields surrounding the building. Its steel rib and cable tie construction were inspired by the traditional shipbuilding technology of the area. Thus, we can see that the wavy roof shaping the entire building and dividing the museum into its three main spaces was inspired by the physical and historical context

Figure 5.3 The context and rhythm of the Zentrum Paul Klee, Bern, Switzerland. From Noemi Pinto/500Px Plus via Getty Images.

of the site, as well as being considered an interpretation of Klee's artistic work (Renzo Piano Building Workshop, n.d.). What makes this wavy roof truly unique, however, is its Rhythm. It is made up of numerous, regularly spaced steel ribs that provide a beautiful example of rhythmic building elements. The regular Rhythm of these ribs creates a language and a rational ruleset to the building, then carries it out visibly. This Rhythm provides the viewer the comfort and stability of knowing that there is a structural rib at every point of expectation. If one were missing, it would throw the entire assembly off balance and into unease. But, as designed, this rhythmic rib structure becomes a beautiful part of the region's topography on the exterior and a powerful organizing system on the interior.

This building incorporates and successfully displays several important design principles. As described in Archjourney (n.d.), "The design of the building and the physiognomy of its space interpret [Klee's] passion for a harmony of form and the proportions of nature." Therefore, this, just as the previously discussed Parthenon and Salk Institute, is considered a great work of fitted and proper architecture because of its rootedness in its Context, and the Story it very successfully tells about Paul Klee through Rhythm, Order, Harmony, and Proportion.

Proportion

Another very commonly sought-after design principle is that of proportion, a vital element of buildings from classical Greece and Rome to the Modern movement. Of proportion, Vitruvius (1960) said, "This is found when the members of a work are of a height suited to their breadth, of a breadth suited to their length, and, in a word, when they all correspond symmetrically." Proportion is another important principle in providing comfort and even beauty. When Proportion is off, it makes the human experience unnatural and distracting. Nature itself provides many examples of the importance and beauty of Proportion. The golden ratio or golden mean is a mathematical proportioning system identified by 5th century B.C. scholar Pythagoras, which we find all over nature, in everything from the design of flower petals to shells to the human face to galaxies. In things we understand as beautiful, the human eye can discern subtle differences of proportionality, intuitively understanding when something is off. In architecture, we see the importance of the golden ratio in ancient examples such as the Parthenon (Figure 5.1), Vaastu principles of the Taj Mahal (Figure 5.5), and other Indian architecture, the standard of the Vitruvian Man of the Renaissance, and Le Corbusier's guiding Modulor Man of modernism.

An amazingly rigorous exploration of this idea of proportion is the Basilica of Santa Maria Novella (Figure 5.4) in Florence, Italy.

Figure 5.4 Front façade of Santa Maria Novella, Florence, Italy. From: Eleonora
Altomare, unsplash.com.

This Medieval church was added to and altered throughout the years. Finally, in the late 15th century, Renaissance architect, theorist, and writer Leon Battista Alberti was commissioned to harmonize the entire collective. Alberti chose to do so through the employment of a strict mathematical proportional system based on the proportional scale of the human body:

> The relationships of the parts amongst themselves and with the entirety are established by a harmonic proportional system derived from simple ratios (one to one, one to two, one to three, etc.), which are at the basis of musical harmony. This system permitted Alberti to define the position and dimension of every element of the facade. The one-to-two relationship governs the composition of the entire facade, which appears inscribed in a square, while a smaller square (with sides equal to half that of the larger square) establishes the relationship between the two floors, breaks up the lower part, and circumscribes the upper central part. This ratio is maintained for all the elements of the facade, so that it appears built geometrically on the basis of a progressive halving or doubling of the measurements, always maintaining the same proportion.
>
> (as cited in Magrini, n.d.)

Proportion is an apparent principle in many examples throughout history that are considered among the world's most beautiful works of architecture, including the Parthenon (Figure 5.1), the Taj Mahal (Figure 5.5), St. Peter's Basilica in Rome (Figure 5.7), the Eiffel Tower in Paris (Figure 3.1), the Unite de Habitation in Marseilles, the CCTV Headquarters in Beijing, and many others.

Group B: Balance, Scale, and Circulation

The next group of Design Principles contribute greatly to the perceived importance, prominence, and formality of a building and therefore to the organization housed therein. We all sense this intrinsically when we approach a government building, cathedral, or civic institution. These are typically large, imposing buildings with prominent, central entries which are often raised up on a pedestal. One often must ascend some steps to enter, proceed through a large entry porch or vestibule, and proceed along a symmetrical path. On the other hand, some buildings are small, unimposing, and easily accessible. These are all intentional characteristics intended to silently communicate powerful messages of power and status. An exploration of the following principles of balance, scale, and circulation and a study of various examples of these principles in action will allow leaders to formulate spaces that achieve similar ends.

Balance and Symmetry

One of the major principles proposed by Vitruvius is that of balance and symmetry. Vitruvius (1960) wrote that, "Symmetry is a proper agreement between the members of the work itself, and relation between the different parts and the whole general scheme, in accordance with a certain part selected as standard." This doesn't necessarily mean that the left half of a building is a mirrored reflection of the right half, but that the major components relate so that the entire assembly seems unified and harmonious. The collection of parts creates balance or symmetry in the way they are assembled into the whole. They create a state of equilibrium resulting in a pleasing composition. Balance depends upon the equal distribution of the visual weights of the architectural and interior elements, where visual weight is a measure of both mass and of how attractive that mass is to the eye.

Symmetrical design is a principle that has seemingly always been associated with formality and therefore, buildings of importance such as governmental buildings, churches, civic institutions, etc. Asymmetry connotes a more casual approach and use, but Balance can be achieved with either approach and is typically a much-desired characteristic.

The Taj Mahal (Figure 5.5) is one of the world's great examples of symmetrical Balance, as well as the principles of Proportion, Harmony, and Scale.

Figure 5.5 Central axial view across the reflecting pool to the Taj Mahal, Agra, Uttar Pradesh, India. From: Shan Elahi, unsplash.com.

The Taj Mahal is a UNESCO World Heritage Site and is considered one of the Seven Wonders of the World. This white marble mausoleum in the Indian city of Agra, designed by the emperor's architect Ustad Ahmad Lahauri and finished in 1643, is the centerpiece of a 42-acre complex set in formal gardens with a very long reflecting pool axially aligned with the building's front door and the grand South Gate. The building is topped by a 115-foot-high central dome, further accentuating the central, axial symmetry. This also establishes the one-to-one proportion of the building in that the height to the top of the dome is equal to the length of the base. The Order, Rhythm, and Proportion of this building give it a great sense of peace, comfort, and beauty, while its symmetrical balance provides a sense of formality, grandness, and importance.

Famed American architect Frank Lloyd Wright's Unity Temple (Figure 5.6) in Oak Park, Illinois, is a beautiful and widely recognized example of asymmetrical Balance.

Wright designed this building in 1905 for a Unitarian Congregation in Oak Park as an early exploration of modern architectural ideas as applied to sacred space. There is an inscription written above the doors to the entrance lobby stating, *For the worship of God and the service of man.* Wright designed the building as two distinct parts representing these two components of life. One part was dedicated to the worship space and one for the offices and operations, dividing the sacred from the profane, the heavenly from the earthly, the worship of God from the service of man, ideas that are not equal, but that need to be balanced in our lives.

Figure 5.6 The asymmetrical balance of the Unity Temple in Oak Park, Illinois. From © 2022 James Caulfield/Caulfield Archive

One enters this building through an entry courtyard and lobby that separates the two main building masses. The large cube of the worship building is offset by the three smaller cubes of the office building. These two masses, though asymmetrical, exist in beautiful balance with each other around the entry court and lobby. The two concepts of relating to God and man are both important parts of a human's existence and are both given due reverence in these building forms. Yet, the importance of God's work over man's is clearly communicated as well. The use of Balance in this building communicates these ideas brilliantly, and the Unity Temple is considered a masterpiece of modern architecture.

Scale

Scale is a principle of which you probably have been, at least at times, aware. Scale can affect how one approaches a building, how one feels upon entering, and how one acts both outside and in. Scale can overwhelm and overcome or can welcome and embrace. This effect can be achieved by the entire building, the exterior spaces related to a building, the interior spaces of a building, or even the arrangement of furniture within a space.

St. Peter's Basilica in Vatican City (Figure 5.7), which we have previously discussed as an example of multiple principles, is a very potent example

Figure 5.7 The front façade of St. Peter's Basilica from the Piazza St. Peter's, Vatican City, Italy. From Alex Folguera, unspash.com.

of the use of scale. St. Peter's is the universal headquarters of the Catholic Church, the residence of the Pope, and the traditional burial place of St. Peter, one of Jesus' 12 chosen disciples. A succession of noted architects, including Michelangelo, Raphael, and Bramante, were tasked with creating a design specifically intended to express this building's importance and the enduring stability and strength of the Catholic Church and faith. It was designed as a building, an interior space, and an urban plan that is unmistakable in its messaging and meaning. It is, in fact, the largest church in the world at 720 feet long, 490 feet wide, and 448 feet tall. Some of the doors are 25 feet high.

St. Peter's Basilica is designed to help the visitor understand that God and the Catholic Church are more important than any single person. The scale of the entrance piazza is massive and reaches well into the surrounding city, making the whole assembly visible from many places across Rome. The interior spaces are equally awe-inspiring. The massive interior space is also filled with some of the world's most famous paintings, sculptures, and stained glass, by artists such as Michelangelo and Bernini. The scale of it all is overwhelming, and that is exactly the point. This building tells its intended story with amazing success. St. Peter's use of scale is so effective that it has become one of the most visited buildings in the world. We see scale used similarly to express religious intentions to great effect in many buildings around the world, such as the Hagia Sophia in Istanbul, the Pashupatinath temple in Kathmandu, and others.

Scale is also used to express the importance of other types of institutions, such as seats of power and governing authorities. Many kings throughout history have ruled from a grand castle or palace, such as Versailles outside of Paris, Buckingham Palace in London, or the Forbidden City in Beijing, built specifically to communicate their position and authority. Democratic governments have traditionally used scale to express their legitimacy and stability in various ways as well. The Foursquare courthouse design in many small Midwest towns across the United States offers a central, imposing building that is often the hub of small-town life, commerce, and governance. This idea was also employed to great effect by America's forefathers in the design of Washington D.C.

To express that the United States was to be governed by the people, the U.S. Capitol Building, the seat of the government and the meeting place for congress, was placed on the highest point of the capital city, 88 feet above the Potomac River, on the central axis of the National Mall. The building itself is over 750 feet long, 350 feet wide, and 288 feet tall (Architect of the Capitol, n.d.). This makes the building visible across the city, even from great distances, much like St. Peter's.

The Capitol building's centrally located entries are raised above the ground and accessible by surmounting a substantial number of stairs both

Figure 5.8 Looking up the steps to the entry to the U.S. Capitol building, Washington D.C. From: Louis Velazquez, unsplash.com.

in the front and back of the building. Ascending to enter a building further emphasizes its importance, grandeur, and authority. The central Rotunda, beneath the impressive dome, rises 180 feet above the floor, overwhelming the scale of a human. The new nation needed an architecture that would communicate the United States' legitimacy and that the United States was deserving of respect, as evidenced by the Capitol's scale, which George Washington admired for "its grandeur" (Architect of the Capitol, n.d.).

The Vietnam War Memorial (Figure 4.9), designed by architect and artist Maya Lin in 1982 and located just down the mall from the U.S. Capitol building in Washington, D.C., employs the principle of scale in an opposite but equally effective way. This project, which consists of one simple, angled wall, and the surrounding landscape, is an example of a part of the built environment that is not an enclosed building but is still designed to be experienced by humans in a very specific way with very specific intentions.

This memorial project was undertaken to establish a place to remember those who served in one of the longest and most controversial military actions in American history, a very tall order.

In her design, Lin sought to create a place for not only remembering, but also for healing. Lin told Bill Moyers in a 2003 interview, "I imagined taking a knife and cutting into the earth, opening it up, with an initial violence

Figure 5.9 Looking down the path into the Vietnam War Memorial, Washington D.C. Photo by Mark A. Roberson.

and pain that in time would heal." Lin's design is very simple, with one long, name-covered wall sloping downward from the ground plane of the mall to a depth of ten feet below grade at its center, rendering it almost invisible until you get to it, never large or impressive or overwhelming like its neighboring memorials and government buildings. It is understated and peaceful, not what one might expect from a war memorial. But it has proven to be one of the most powerfully effective war memorials the United States has ever built. If you have visited the memorial, you know how true this is. In 2007, the AIA awarded this project with its Twenty-five Year Award, recognizing that even very quiet, restrained architecture could employ the principle of scale to inspire and even heal.

Circulation/Transition/Boundary

Circulation is a principle that everyone experiences daily but is often not consciously considered. It's an element that is typically only noticed when it doesn't work well. One might be able to better visualize the idea of circulation in other contexts, such as the movement of traffic through a city or:

The movement of blood around the human body. In architecture, the concept of circulation isn't so different – it refers to the way people, the blood of our buildings, move through space. In particular, circulation routes are the pathways people take through and around buildings or urban places. Circulation is often thought of as the 'space between the spaces', having a connective function, but it can be much more than that. It is the concept that captures the experience of moving our bodies around a building, three-dimensionally and through time.

(portico.space, n.d.)

Circulation consists of getting into, moving through, and understanding the arrangement of a building.

When the circulatory path is well designed, you can find your way into and through a building without thinking too much about what you're doing. However, when circulation is done poorly, you notice quickly. Some components of circulation are more obvious, such as walking down a hall, moving through a room, or climbing a set of stairs. However, other important components of the experience of circulation are less obvious, such as the transition from one space, use, or condition to another. Moving from outside to in, from public to private, from light to dark, or loud to quiet, is what prepares us to then move through a space, as guided by the provided thresholds and boundaries. Well thought out circulation, in all its parts, is vital for a building to be considered great.

The Guggenheim Museum (Figure 5.10) in New York City, designed by Frank Lloyd Wright, is a project in which the circulation path is the central organizing idea of the whole building.

Wright envisioned visitors entering the main space on the ground floor, ascending to the top of the building via elevator, and then slowly spiraling around the main central space as one descends the ¼ mile-long ramp which accommodates the actual viewing of the resident art, and finally completing the journey back at the ground floor of the main space where the trek began. Architect and Frank Lloyd Wright apprentice Bruce Brooks Pfeiffer (as cited in Lifson, 2009) said that Wright's vision for the circulatory experience included: "Let[ting] the elevator do the lifting so the visitor could do the drifting."

Museums traditionally featured central circulation with galleries on one or both sides prior to the design of the Guggenheim, such as at the Louvre, the Uffizi, and many others. But the Guggenheim gives the center to the grand, soaring, sky-lit space. And by creating circulation around the edge of this space and only allowing access to the edge on the ground floor before and after one actually encounters and views the art, Wright completely separates the act of viewing art from the experience of occupying the grand space. Paul Goldberger (as cited in Lifson, 2009), former architecture critic

Figure 5.10 The grand interior atrium of Guggenheim Museum, New York, NY. From: Nicholas Ceglia, unsplash.com.

for The New Yorker, wrote that this building proved, "That there are other ways to show art than in a neutral space. That an architect can do something that's powerful in itself and that enhances the experience of looking at art." The Guggenheim, awarded the AIA Twenty-five Year Award in 1986, thereby changed how we consider the act of viewing art by the simple and intentional employment of a system of circulation.

A vital component of circulation systems are the transitions – between outside and inside, between public and private, between one use and another. How one crosses a boundary determines the ease and comfort of doing so. Disneyland Park (Figure 4.11) does this very intentionally, as one transitions into the park from the entrance, through the tunnels under the railroad, and then from one land to another, such as from Adventureland to Frontierland and now through another tunnel to the new Star Wars: Galaxy's Edge. Part of Disney's success at this comes from the original park designers' experience in movies and TV, where they gained an appreciation and expertise in the art of the cross-dissolve. In fact, in the book Walt and the Promise of Progress City by Sam Gennawey (2013), Walt Disney was cited as saying that a cross-dissolve in a film:

Figure 5.11 Example of Engawa in a traditional Japanese house. From Cellai Stefano/EyeEm via Getty Images.

Superimposes the tail end of the first clip on the beginning of the second clip, and fades the clips in and out. When done correctly, the effect moves the story along while the audience barely notices the transition. When done poorly, it jars the viewer.

In traditional Japanese houses, there is a space of *engawa*, which is a space that is considered both inside and outside, designed to facilitate the idea that one needs to have the time and space to transition between the outside and inside worlds physically and emotionally.

The lack of such spaces in contemporary American homes reduces our opportunity to make such a transition gracefully. Even such a simple thing has a profound effect. How one moves into a building from the outside and then through the building from one experience to another is an often forgotten yet crucial opportunity to enhance the successful circumnavigation of the story that the building is telling.

Group C: Harmony, Color, and Sensory Engagement

The last group of Design Principles are those meant to heighten our senses and move us from the ordinary and mundane to something special. These

Design Principles communicate messages of peace, reflection, contemplation, inspiration, and even excitement and joy. You may have had the experience of entering a building that affected you emotionally and caused you to fall silent or created a desire to sing or to feel joyful. These examples demonstrate how the physical environment can similarly affect those who experience it. Harmony, color, and sensory engagement contribute to a person's lived experience of a space.

Harmony

Harmony is an effect we have mentioned many times and is the result of the correct application of many of these previously mentioned principles. Harmony results from context and story, and is part of a building's fittedness.

As was discussed, the Kaufmann House at Bear Run, Pennsylvania, or Fallingwater (Figure 4.5), is an example of a building that emerged from its Context. Two of the elements relating to Context are also part of what makes Fallingwater an amazing example of harmony. When presented with the site by the Kaufmanns, a site that was greatly beloved by the client and a place that they frequented for hikes and picnics, Frank Lloyd Wright was faced with a dilemma of how to place a house on this beautiful location that would make it seem like a piece of the natural site that had always been there, taking full advantage of the river and the waterfall.

Wright decided to do something unexpected and bold yet ultimately harmonious with the site. Instead of placing the house in a location that would afford it views of the river and waterfall, he designed the house to sit right on top of the waterfall, such that the moving water becomes an integral element of the house as it runs under and around the structure. The river's site, sound, and feel are now an ever-present element of the house, harmonizing the two together in ways that make the house seem like a part of the landscape carved out by the moving waters. Also, the color and form of the house harmonize beautifully with the naturally horizontal ledges of stone that are such a prominent feature of the site.

The U.S. Air Force Academy Cadet Chapel (Figure 5.12), just north of Colorado Springs, Colorado, was designed by SOM Architects and completed in 1962. This is a building that harmonizes with its natural site, but even more so with its history, users, and purpose.

The site is a sloping piece of land in the middle of the U.S. Air Force Academy campus. Mountains surround the campus, as it sits very near the majestic Rocky Mountain Range. There is then a relationship between the natural context and the chapel's soaring, 150-foot-tall spires. However, those angular, pointed, wing-like stainless steel spires refer much more directly to the campus' purpose, which is to train officers for the U.S. Air Force. The spires are reminiscent of fighter jet wings in particular and

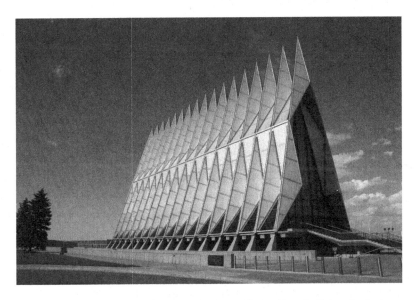

Figure 5.12 United States Air Force Academy Cadet Chapel, Colorado Springs, CO. From: Laura Gangi Pond, shutterstock.com.

advanced, space-age aviation in general. The spires point to the sky above, which is the province of the Air Force, and they create an interior space that is all about looking up and being inspired by height, space, and beautiful, multicolored light, reminiscent of a sunset. There are 17 of these metallic spires that create a very effective rhythm as they are separated by stained glass windows.

This building is designed such that its references to combat aircraft doesn't take away from the beauty and peace of the worship space housed within. The building's references to its place and users are harmonized beautifully with its purpose. This is also a very balanced, even symmetrical building, and to enter the main chapel space you must ascend several steps to an entry deck from which you enter the chapel through a centrally located door. The combination of all of these Design Principles creates a beautifully harmonious and iconic building that seems perfectly fitted for its place and purpose – so much so that in 1996 the AIA awarded the building its Twenty-five Year award, and in 2004, the building was named a U.S. National Historic Landmark.

Color

Colors in a painting or photograph can help an image project a certain mood. In the same way, colors used in architecture can profoundly influence how people using or viewing it feel in response. Thus, color is an integral element of great architecture worldwide. According to St. Clair (2017), author of *The Secret Lives of Color*, "Color is fundamental to our experience of the world." Color is used to inspire as it dramatically pierces the darkness of Notre-Dame du Haut at Ronchamp, France, or the Sagrada Familia in Barcelona, Spain (Figure 5.13). It is also used to draw attention to and identify the exposed structure and building systems at the Pompidou Center in Paris, France. It is used to create spaces of peace and calm, as well as to express cultural identity in the Casa Luis Barragan in Mexico City, Mexico, or the Latino Cultural Center in Dallas, Texas.

Studies show that different colors influence our thoughts, feelings, and moods differently (Babin et al., 2003). For example, Health Harvard (2020) reported that blue light slows the production of melatonin, keeping people more alert or awake even at night. Understanding the influence of color and employing colors intentionally can be an important part of creating an environment communicating desired culture and values.

Perhaps no physical environment in the world takes such careful pains to employ color to accomplish specific purposes as Disneyland Park (Figure 4.11), particularly in the way color is used as a storytelling device. John Hench (2009) stated, "We know that color is a direct experience: people see color, and they feel color's emotional effects. What really matters is that color provides an extraordinary expressive means for communicating ideas" (p. 103). Disney's Imagineers have given much thought and attention to the meaning and effects of each color in the palate, from the solid, strong, earthy browns of Big Thunder Mountain Railroad to the warm, attention-grabbing red of the Plaza Inn on Main Street to the reassuring, life-giving blue of Sleeping Beauty's Castle to the abundance, rest and leisure of the green landscaping that surrounds everything in the park (all adjectives from John Hench and Designing Disney). Disney even developed two colors called *Go Away Green* and *Blending Blue* to paint things they do not want guests to notice, such as trash cans, mechanical equipment, construction fences, and even the door to the exclusive Club 33, a private club and executive lounge.

Color is a powerful physiological and psychological tool and a Design Principle that is vital to communicating intended messages as a leader. If you want employees to be inspired, creative, and high-energy but then use a restful or boring color scheme, you will be inhibiting your purpose from the beginning. Understanding the powerful effects of color in the way that Disney does can make a great difference in the success of your space. Color is a particularly effective Design Principle inducing physiological, therapeutic, and energetic effects (Day, 2014).

Figure 5.13 Interior side aisle lit up with colored light streaming in through the stained-glass windows of the Sagrada Familia, Barcelona, Spain. Photo courtesy of Keelan Kaiser.

Sensory Engagement

The engagement of all of our senses is an often-overlooked way for architecture to affect us in powerful and worthwhile ways. And when we think about it, sensory engagement is happening around us all the time, whether intentional or not.

We see clearly that a built environment like Disneyland Park is so thoroughly successful because every element of the site and experience was carefully considered and designed to communicate desired messages and to create conditions for a culture of *The Happiest Place on Earth*. Those conditions include everything you see, hear, touch, and even smell, and where and how you circulate into and through the park. John Hench (2009) stated, "Once inside [Disneyland] guests find themselves in a place full of heightened color, bright flowers, soft music, pleasant smells, and activity all around" (p. 65). All of this is done in service of the Story, which springs from and continues the Context of Walt Disney's life and experience, and ultimately creates a three-dimensional built environment that seems more fitted to its place and time than anything else in Anaheim, California. According to Hench (2009), "Mood sensation and creating an enhanced reality are aspects of storytelling that we translate into three-dimensional design through theming and form" (p. 56).

A much earlier but highly effective example of this multi-sensory engagement is the previously referenced Mosaic Tabernacle (Figure 3.3). As one advanced through the carefully planned circulation system, one would feed wood to a fire, feeling the experience of warmth; wash their hands with cool, enveloping water; smell incense; and taste the sacramental bread; seeing the elements of fire, darkness, and then light, proceeding from external noise to silence within the holy place, all laid out in minute detail in the Old Testament Book of Exodus. This intense engagement of human senses prepares one for the ultimate moment of entering the "holy of holies" and being in the presence of God.

Church of the Light (Figure 5.14), completed in 1989 in Ibaraki, Japan, by architect Tadao Ando, is a stark, bare, concrete structure in which the only decoration or relief is the light streaking into the end of the nave through slits in the concrete that create a cross.

The concrete is completely smooth and even cold to the touch, the space is very quiet, and the experience is engulfed in darkness. The journey through this space begins in almost total darkness and silence, which is only broken by the cross bringing in welcome light. Architect Kroll (n.d.) described Ando's Church of the Light by saying, "The intersection of light and solid raises the occupant's awareness of the spiritual and secular within themselves." The use of dark, light, and material in this project heightens

Figure 5.14 Interior image of the main interior space of the Church of the Light, Ibaraki, Japan. From: Sira Anamwong, shutterstock.com.

the visitor's awareness of every sound they make, elevating the experience of silence and sound within the space as well. Overall, Ando uses Balance, Proportion, Order, color (the intentionally complete lack thereof), and sensory engagement to communicate exactly the message, norms, and culture desired.

Chapter Summary

When employed knowingly and intentionally, applied Design Principles can take simple Building Elements and elevate them to the level of inspiration, enlightenment, culture creation, and delight. A practical but important thought to keep in mind is that despite the large budgets and resources of many of these examples, good design and the application of these design principles is scalable. More important than big budgets and seemingly unending resources is the thoughtful, attentive, and intentional design process by which architects and leaders design. You can employ the art and science of architecture, exercising architectural license to optimize the messaging of workplaces, new or inherited, just as intentionally as these many examples did, masterworks and otherwise. Senior Design Researcher for

Steelcase, Inc. Melanie Redman (2017) summed up her research on the interaction between people and their workplace, stating that:

> Time and again our studies have shown the role that physical space can play in encouraging the behaviours and outcomes organisations want to see in the workplace, including resiliency, agility, employee engagement and wellbeing. In this vein, leadership spaces can be used to send a message regarding how an organisation works and its values, while simultaneously helping [leaders] to do their job in the best way possible.
>
> (p. 2)

Building Elements and Design Principles are two essential and closely related components of great architecture and are demonstrated by the many examples described herein. However, our proposed Critical Components of Architecture triangle cannot exist completely or successfully without the thorough incorporation of the third leg, which is Use Strategies.

References

Architect of the Capitol. (n.d.). *U.S. capital building.* www.aoc.gov/explore-capitol-campus/buildings-grounds/capitol-building

Archjourney.org. (n.d.). *Paul Klee Zentrum.* https://archjourney.org/projects/paul-klee-zentrum/

Babin, B. J., Hardesty, D. M., & Suter, T. A. (2003). Color and shopping intentions: The intervening effect of price fairness and perceived affect. *Journal of Business Research, 56*(7), 541–551. https://doi.org/10.1016/S0148-2963(01)00246-6

Collins, J. C. (2001). *Good to great: Why some companies make the leap – And others don't.* HarperBusiness.

Day, C. (2014). *Places of the soul: Architecture and environmental design as healing art* (3rd ed.). Routledge.

Gennawey, S. (2013). *Disneyland story: The Unofficial guide to the evolution of Walt Disney's dream.* Unofficial Guides.

Harvard Health Publishing. (2020). *Blue light has a dark side.* www.health.harvard.edu/staying-healthy/blue-light-has-a-dark-side

Hench, J. (2009). *Designing Disney: Imagineering and the art of the show (A Walt Disney Imagineering Book).* Disney Editions.

Kroll, A. (n.d.). *AD classics: Church of the Light/Tadao Ando Architect & Associates.* www.archdaily.com/101260/ad-classics-church-of-the-light-tadao-ando

Lifson, E. (2009, August 5). Guggenheim Museum: The spiral that broke all the rules. *NPR.* www.npr.org/2009/08/05/130274408/guggenheim-museum-the-spiral-that-broke-all-the-rules

Lin, M., & Moyers, B. (2003). *Interview with Maya Lin on becoming American: The Chinese experience.* Public Affairs Television. www.pbs.org/becomingamerican/ap_pjourneys_transcript5.html

Magrini, G. (n.d.). *Basilica of Santa Maria Novella.* https://brunelleschi.imss.fi.it/itineraries/place/BasilicaOfSantaMariaNovella.html

portico.space. (n.d.). *What is circulation?* http://portico.space/journal//architectural-concepts-circulation#:~:text=In%20architecture%2C%20the%20concept%20of,around%20buildings%20or%20urban%20places

Redman, M. (2017). *Designing spaces for the connected leader.* www.management-issues.com/opinion/7265/designing-spaces-for-the-connected-leader/

Renzo Piano Building Workshop. (n.d.). *Zentrum Paul Klee.* https://arquitectur-aviva.com/works/zentrum-paul-klee-berna-3

St. Clair, K. (2017). *The secret lives of color.* Penguin Books.

Sullivan, L. H. (1896). *The tall office building artistically considered.* https://ocw.mit.edu/courses/4-205-analysis-of-contemporary-architecture-fall-2009/e9f665db203bf5acb2ce44d91f75b66e_MIT4_205F09_Sullivan.pdf

Vitruvius. (1960). *The Ten books on architecture* (M. H. Morgan, Trans.). Dover Publications (Original work published 1914).

6 Leadership and Use Strategies

Introduction

We have firmly established that a major part of our human experience is living relationally with our built environment, an experience that influences us, often without our being able to fully articulate how. For example, in the 1990s, I (Alicia) worked on the second floor of an office building – a large rectangular room filled with beige, ten-foot cubicle walls. None of the workers had window view access since the exterior walls were reserved for the leadership team. While in that space, I found myself fatigued, antsy, bored, lacking initiative, qualities that weren't typically part of my behavior, and I struggled within that space. In contrast, when I worked in a decorated conference room with color and window views, I was energized. That experience and others like it drew me to explore how the physical design of a space influences people and how leaders might consider the built environment as part of their overall suite of strategies.

In the preceding chapters, we addressed the first two legs of our Critical Components of Architecture triangle, and we now will tackle the third leg, Use Strategies. An intentionally articulated suite of Use Strategies considers those human and architectural values pertinent to the organization. This chapter aims to lay out a process for understanding and establishing a successful Use Strategy. However, to get to that end goal, an organization must thoroughly understand itself – who it is, who it wants to be, and how it wants others to see and experience it. We propose several steps that an organization can follow to achieve this essential level of self-awareness. First, we will describe the underlying factors shaping an organizational context, including identity, culture, climate, and structure. These factors are then translated into specific human and architectural values, including contribution, community, collaboration, creativity, and communication, which will influence the determination of appropriate Use Strategies, leading to better architectural decision making in terms of Building Elements and Design Principles.

DOI: 10.4324/9781003166788-6

Exploring architecture and leadership is an interdisciplinary experience moving beyond utilitarian functionality, related to how we want to use a space via understanding the relationships between the built environment, context, organizational identity, culture, climate, and structure. Considered together, architecture and leadership can foster vibrant spaces influencing identity and, sense of belonging. These spaces afford opportunities to, a space to relate dialogically, co-creatively participating in creating and holding meaningful space.

The built environment within which leadership occurs can be interrogated to determine leadership influences, biases, and values translated into overall design, how boundaries define space and wield power, and how people live within and experience the context. Ropo et al. (2015) noted four trends in organizational space studies: (a) studies of the physical environment; (b) subjective or phenomenological exploring of lived experiences; (c) critical approaches emphasizing power, politics, and control; and the emergent approach (d) esthetic perspectives. These approaches all contribute to a clearer picture of organizational context wherein people live and work.

Context involves those tangible and intangible factors influencing people. People need to "see how other 'things' in our environment lead us, such as architectural, design, and layout solutions, physical objects, artifacts, and even city-spaces" (Ropo et al., 2015, p. 2). An organizational context includes the built environment, history, identity, culture, politics, economics, etc., wherein a dialogically reciprocal relationship exists between organizational context and leadership. The term *dialogically reciprocal* simply means there is a give and take between multiple aspects external and internal to an organization. A natural example of this is found within conversation among friends where one person speaks, another adds, someone laughs, another interjects a line, etc. We experience a conversation communally where everyone participating has a part and contributes to the overall experience of the conversation. It's in thinking about the qualities contributing to a natural relational ebb and flow affirming each person's participation that we imagine when we think of the intersection between architecture and leadership. Further, the built environment shapes our identity, sense of self, interactions, and agency. The ways people experience, make sense of, and assign meaning to their context are illustrated by four distinct but interrelated concepts: organizational identity, organizational culture, organizational climate, and organizational structure.

Organizational Identity

Identity, in general, is made up of those factors that express who we are uniquely and distinctly. Organizational identity is influenced by an organization's name (who we are), mission (what we do), target audience (who we serve), reputation (espoused and enacted values), and overall brand as communicated by things like logo, stories, website, architecture, and other symbols. The layering of various identities, symbols, and articulations of who we are contribute to how others perceive us. For example, at one time, IBM mandated that their employees wore a white shirt, black tie, and dark gray suit as part of their identity and branding. In contrast, the consulting firm I worked for allowed casual attire. Our firm stood out against the more formal dress and attitudes of IBM. How each was perceived depended on the perceiver's values. A person associating formal dress with professionalism, competence, and skills would likely gravitate toward IBM; however, associations of casual dress as those being ready to work and get their hands dirty often translated into our being hired. This dress code illustration works the same way with architecture. The built environment reflects our identity, communicating our values to employees, visitors, and customers. Organizational theorists Hatch and Schultz (2002) described the interplay between identity, culture, and image as expressing who we are translated into organizational culture, which ultimately leaves impressions on others.

Organizational Culture

Behaviors emerging from cultural values and norms display themselves without our thinking about them or even necessarily being able to articulate what those values or norms are explicitly. Organizational culture was defined by organizational theorist Edgar Schein (2010) as:

> Pattern[s] of shared basic assumptions learned by a group as it solved its problems of external adaptation and internal integration, which has worked well enough to be considered valid and; therefore, to be taught to new members as the correct way to perceive, think, and feel in relation to those problems.
>
> (p. 18)

Our behaviors become habitual and provide meaning in the way they enable us to make sense of the world. We quickly assess what the context is and what behaviors are required given that context. For example, when we enter a hospital or a rock concert venue, we know the expected behaviors within each space, given our knowledge of cultural and social norms within the specific context.

When describing explicit behaviors, we are likely to hear phrases like: *this is the way we do things*, or *we've always done it like this* to describe the rationale for any given behavior. Norms and values represent shared agreements for desirable behavior, helping people to distinguish *should* and *ought*, telegraphing to others what it means to conform or fit into the social group. Beliefs are basic assumptions about the nature of truth. These beliefs are learned, deeply ingrained, often explicitly unknown, and unquestioned. Schein (2010) proposed three levels to culture: Level 1 artifacts, Level 2 espoused beliefs and values, and Level 3 basic underlying assumptions. Rather than being three separate distinct categories, these three levels work interactively, dialogically, to create culture in a unique contextual way.

Specifically, Level 1 artifacts refer to the "visible and feelable structures and processes" (p. 24) within a context, but understanding the artifacts requires understanding espoused beliefs and values. In this sense, architecture is a critical contributor to organizational culture. Schein then referred to organizational climate as "the *feeling* (emphasis added) that is conveyed . . . by the physical layout." Organizational culture and climate were distinguished by Barbera and Schneider (2014), wherein, culture represents the *values and beliefs* transmitted by socialization, decision making, and myths and stories, and climate is the *meaning* people attach to policies, practices, and behaviors.

Organizational Climate

Organizational climate explores the "meaning employees attach to the policies, practices, and procedures they experience and the behaviors they observe being rewarded, supported and expected" (Schneider et al., 2013, p. 381). Organizational climate is the way people experience and interpret a space. For example, early in my career, I worked on a consulting contract on a job site at a nuclear power plant. People working directly for the utility worked in a nicely appointed office, whereas our team was situated in a trailer supplied with discarded mismatched furniture, worn floors, and no attempt at esthetics. We experienced dissonance in the way our boss interacted with us (espoused values) and the workspace (enacted values). A person saying, *this place gives me the creeps, I don't feel like I can share openly here*, etc., are other examples of this. Responding to a place's climate is representative of one's experiences or feelings within a space. Organizational climate, then, is illustrative of a "conglomerate of attitudes, feelings, and behaviors, which characterizes the life in the organization" (Ekvall & Ryhammar, 1998, p. 126).

Ekvall (1987), who identified ten dimensions of organizational climate enabling creativity and innovation within organizations, noted how "Climate affects organizational and psychological processes such as communication, problem solving, decision making, conflict handling, learning and motivation . . . The individual is affected by the climate as a whole, by the general psychological atmosphere." Ekvall and Ryhammar (1999) found that leaders described their role as creating atmosphere and that resources such as technology, physical space, etc., influence climate. The physical space is a key contributor to creating the atmosphere or feel of a place, influencing people's interactions and the way activities are conducted.

We now turn to unpacking organizational structure as an overt articulation of how work is conceived (differentiation and integration), variables affecting structure, and organizational design.

Organizational Structure

Organizational structure plays an important role in an overall organizational context, and in the capacity to respond to emergent scenarios. Consider the organization chart where you lead. At its simplest, organizational structure is about how people are grouped to accomplish work in coordinated and structured ways to achieve organizational goals. Designing an organizational structure is influenced by an organization's purpose, history, culture, and personalities, changing over time. While there is no single way to organize, organizational structure is important in the way structure influences expectations, norms, and exchanges among people.

Structural *form* both enhances and constrains what is possible and what an organization can accomplish. Organizational form is important for humans and the built environment within which we organize. Organizational theorists Bolman and Deal (2013) specifically used the word *architecture* to describe the importance of organizational structure as a type of "social architecture." Their usage of the term architecture is significant to our discussion about architecture and leadership, given that the physical architecture influences the social architecture, wherein we are talking about a conscious design of the built environment that encourages the desired social behaviors within the space. The built environment affords physical structure but also significantly contributes to social structures such as one's sense of contribution, creativity, collaboration, communication, sense of community, and overall contextual experience. An easy way to think about organizational structure is to look at your organizational chart which reflects how work is organized while simultaneously communicating a great deal about leadership, organizational culture, and climate.

Critical to an organizational structure is to balance a number of tensions: multifaceted complexity, geographically distributed teams, allocation of differentiated work, and coordination and integration of diverse efforts and work priorities. Each facet of organizational structure offers unique challenges such as coordinating and aligning vision, priorities, responsibilities, work practices, and decision making. For example, maintenance planners in hard offices located in a separate building from maintenance workers may experience coordination and communication difficulties based on proximal differences and the absence of ad hoc meetings such as what often happens around the coffee pot. Their capacity to interact may be further impeded if collaborative spaces are absent or if those spaces are small and lacking access to needed information such as large drawings or vendor manuals. Or, purchasing agents located separate from the physical plant with little connection to plant employees, may lead plant workers to feel as though purchasing agents are *out of touch*. Or, plant monitoring instrumentation and controls staff physically located with information technology in a building distant from plant operators, may impede routine discussions about needed updates to software and hardware. There are many examples of how structure, location, and physical design potentially influences people's ability to interact.

Factors influenced by physical design and arrangement include coordination, workflow, information flow, collaboration, and communication, rising in importance as we consider the organizational structure, physical design, and the way work is performed. Organizations integrate and coordinate work maintaining optimal operations using both *vertical* (formal chains of command; rules and policies, and governance), and *lateral* (meetings, committees, coordinating roles, and network structures) means. Rules, policies, and standards are integral to operations in the way they communicate expectations about work performance and provide a basis for comparability, such that the same task done in separate divisions is done the same way. Lateral coordination refers to the informal ways work gets done, often more agile and ad hoc, lateral means are responsive to organizational needs. For example, an ad hoc, interdisciplinary team is formed to explore reasons for delayed decision making related to a process. The flexibility of the built environment to facilitate this sort of ad hoc gathering, communication, and collaboration is key. Meetings are often the way work is performed laterally but informal contacts (e.g., coffee or lunch conversations) are equally, and sometimes more, important. Our built environment needs to consider formal spaces (offices, meeting rooms) and also informal spaces for interaction, communication, and connection (e.g., lunchrooms, coffee pots, outdoor spaces, etc.).

In thinking about physical design, a goal is to facilitate opportunities for people to get to know each other and to communicate frequently both formally and informally. Ad hoc teams are often formed in response to new problems or opportunities requiring increased collaboration and specific expertise. Coordinating roles are those individuals or groups who use persuasion and personal influence across groups to help coordinate, communicate, and increase opportunity for understanding, shared norms, and standards.

Lateral communication and interactions are enhanced through flexible physical configurations where people can collaborate and connect. An example of this could be a physical open space, with moveable tables and chairs, so a team with representatives from each department can meet in various ways.

Most organizations rely on a combination of vertical and lateral coordination depending on the circumstance. Vertical coordination is suitable for those environments that are stable or predictable with well understood processes. A challenge with vertical coordination, particularly related to the built environment, is the way the architecture may stifle collaboration, creativity, and innovation. For example, leadership offices with doors or on a different floor create a sense of boundary, reducing the amount of communication and the opportunity for informal conversations combined with a perceived experience of fixed-ness versus innovativeness. Lateral coordination is necessary for those complex environments with more variables, risk, and interdependent process and/or information connections. For example, a co-located multidisciplinary maintenance management team (i.e., instrumentation and controls, electrical, and mechanical) can more effectively, efficiently, and creatively respond to equipment failures, therein eliminating delays and reducing emergency downtime. The built environment is the container within which an organizational structure is adopted and enacted and where people strive to do their work. Organizational structure also influences greatly an organization's culture and climate.

Leadership Challenges

An organizational identity, culture, climate, and structure reflectively communicates what an organization looks like and how it functions. It is at the human level that we learn how an organization works and how the context supports work performance and people's lived experiences within a space.

Architecture's historical trajectory reflects biases and assumptions about the human person. For example, Ropo et al. (2015) specifically noted an early connection between leadership, space and place, functionality and scientific management principles put forth by Frederick W. Taylor, a mechanical engineer who influenced organizational design and leadership perspectives. So too, organizational theorists Bolman and Deal (2013) described Taylor's influence where organizations were designed for "maximum efficiency." Organizational structures were often hierarchical and functionally arranged using a cellular approach typically mirroring the organization chart. For example, supervisors in a garment factory had built offices with windows near the front of the factory; whereas the production areas were arranged in a block format related to production sequence and quality assurance. People were co-located depending on their role within the organization chart.

As leadership philosophies changed from hierarchical and bureaucratic toward more participative and collaborative, Morrell et al. (2006) of the Commission for Architecture and the Built Environment and the British Council for Offices observed shifts in organization space design toward more open space plans undergirded with the philosophy of allowing more flexibility. Group offices were designed to facilitate increased interaction, teamwork, communication, and collaboration. For example, a shift from rooms filled with high walled cubicles to a room with individual desks surrounding conference tables with moveable chairs. Some argue that the pendulum swung too far from the 1980s cubicles to the more recent open collaborative workspaces. This change jeopardizes a person's sense of privacy, given that a person is rarely alone, leaving a person feeling like they do not have a designated place and of being over exposed (Congdon et al., 2014). For example, a person saying, *I cannot hear myself think* might be responding to this lack of quiet and privacy.

With Covid-19 and the movement of work to home offices, the rise of "virtual" offices introduces additional challenges to our conceptualization of organizations. The term hybrid office was descriptively used to represent a move "from workplace to culture space" (Fayard et al., 2021). Researchers from New York University Tandon School of Engineering, Fayard et al. (2021) noted, "Pre-pandemic, most businesses saw the office as a place where individuals could get work done. Post-pandemic, the office will only secondarily be a place to carry out tasks or engage in routine meetings." This move represents a shift toward home being the place where individuals do independent tasks and work becomes "primarily a culture space, providing workers with a social anchor, facilitating connections, enabling learning, and fostering unscripted, innovative collaboration" (Fayard et al., 2021). While technological capabilities enhance virtual communication and collaboration, the need for face-to-face is vital to people's wellbeing and organizational culture. In an HBR Ideacast on workplace design, Fayard (Beard & Fayard, 2021) described the importance of having access to physical offices as vital for culture building, socialization, learning by observation, and informal conversations that occur through face-to-face interactions. Physical features like lounge areas, cafeterias, and collaboration space rise in importance to support a hybrid office approach.

Coordinating and leading a complex organization toward organizational mission and goals is a difficult and wondrous task for leadership. Several symptoms suggest an organizational structure including the built environment may need revisiting:

- Differentiation versus integration challenges including: delays in decision making, inconsistent policy interpretation, differing priorities, and role or responsibilities confusion.

- Planning and coordination challenges including: delays, poor communication, unreliability, unresponsiveness, duplication, redundancy, lost data, inflexibility, and poor morale.
- Communication challenges stemming from coordination issues. Communication problems include inconsistent messages, incorrect or incomplete information, lack of communication, unclear expectations, inconsistent planning, decrease in collaboration, and lack of openness. Communication can be hampered due to distributed physical locations and/or lack of connection opportunities.
- Gap and overlap problems such that important work falls through the cracks or and instances where roles overlap creating conflict, wasted effort, and redundancy.
- Siloed operations include symptoms characterized by poor decision making, decreases in efficiency and productivity, increased errors due to lack of coordination, us versus them thinking, lack of communication, it's not my job thinking, and lack of problem identification.
- High attrition numbers may indicate a lack of morale or a lack of value and identity congruence.

These symptoms may adversely impact morale and commitment to organizational goals and may create an undue risk scenario in terms of meeting regulatory requirements. Barnhart-Hoffman (as cited in Steelcase, 2016) observed, "Physical space can encourage resiliency, agility and employee engagement. It can support learning, amplify performance and wellbeing. Or, it can isolate leaders and reinforce silos, and exacerbate stress." Any of these symptoms suggest an opportunity to assess organizational structure including supporting architecture and the built environment to determine opportunities for the physical environment to better reflect values and the work needed to be done.

Articulating Human and Architectural Values

Leaders engage in a balancing act of advancing an organizational mission, meeting organizational goals and objectives, and supporting and guiding employees. When their organization experiences symptoms, leaders experience this acutely as they try to figure out what to do. Often these symptoms point to challenges related to organizational identity, culture, climate, or structure within their architectural context.

Exploring architecture as an active organizational participant influentially supports our efforts to balance objectives including social and human experiences within a context. Decisions about architecture influence organizational identity, culture, climate, and structure. Organizational self-awareness is an important influencer of architectural design in the way our decisions represent deeply held values about brand and identity, reflectively answering the question of who we are as an organization. Cruikshank and Malcolm (1994) stated, "Self-awareness equips a company and its architects to understand the intangible qualities that need to be expressed in bricks and steel" (p. 20). Organizational values and the ways leadership communicates those values contributively shape organizational identity, culture, climate, and structure – affecting the way an organization is experienced.

Articulating values is important in the way our espoused values (what leaders say) focus our attention on what is important. For example, if leadership says we value learning, then they should talk about it, allocate budget toward learning, encourage people to take advantage of learning opportunities, and then reward those who learn and grow – the entire organization as a whole will see and understand the importance of learning as a core value because the leadership espoused messages and actions support and represent the value. *The Dao* or *Way* was described by philosopher and scholar Slingerland (2014) as a "sense of being at home in some framework of values" (p. 15). Ultimately, a person who sees their place in relation to the mission, vision, and values of an organization will experience a part to whole, a connection to something greater (Slingerland, 2014).

Leadership should consider architectural design carefully and mindfully, as a vital part to the whole. A starting point may be for you to intentionally identify critical human values that you deem necessary for your organization, which emerge as a result of understanding your organizational context. Compare those identified human values with the values demonstrated in your built environment. Think of this exercise as overtly articulating your identity (how you want to be seen or experienced) in terms of employees and customers, how you want to work, and how you want those who use your space to feel and experience the space. Keep in mind that each organization has unique values (whether spoken or not) and there may be more values than what we address.

To make sense of our research, we asked an *if this then what* question relative to human values to create 21 corresponding architectural values (Table 6.1). For example, if a human value associated with creativity is balancing the need for collaboration with the need for privacy and working independently, an associated architectural value is to ensure that the physical design incorporates community and private spaces.

Human values influence relationships of individuals with their peers, team or department, organizational leaders, and with the organization as a whole in relation to context. The literature consistently identified six human values: contribution, community, creativity, collaboration, communication, and context.

Table 6.1 Human and Architectural Values

Human Value	Architectural Value
Contribution	• Our physical design process will include participation, contribution, and choice afforded to people who will use the space. • Our physical design will enhance individual and collective contribution by ensuring that people have an esthetically pleasing, flexible environment combined with the appropriate resources, tools, and access to information. • The physical space will actively promote health and well-being.
Community	• Our physical design will be welcoming. • Our physical design will communicate our identity and values. • Our physical design will include informal spaces for conversation and relational connectedness. • Our physical design will open up to and provide connection opportunities to the surrounding community
Collaboration	• Our physical space will flexibly change and adjust to support formal and informal conversations and working together. • Our physical design will include multiple and varied opportunities for meeting and gathering. • Our physical design will include a high level of transparency.
Creativity	• Our physical design will incorporate physical spaces that balance privacy and freedom from distractions with community spaces designed to increase ad hoc interaction, thought, and exploration. • Our physical design will provide access to natural light for all. • Our physical design will include lines of sight to nature and inspiring art, photography, and graphics. • Our physical design will include multi-sensory experiences.
Communication	• Our physical design will represent a participative open approach to leadership where voices are heard and represented. • Our physical design will incorporate lines and shapes that afford differing interactions and contexts for interaction and communication. • Our physical design will include accessible lines of sight to personnel at all administrative levels.
Context	• Our physical design will reflect the local context, history, and culture. • Our physical design will be esthetically pleasing adding to the landscape of esthetic value. • Our physical design will reflect our commitment to and enhance our reputation for care and protection of the environment • Our physical design will maximize people's access to and participation in nature, light, and the environment.

Contribution

At the heart of the human spirit is a desire to lead a meaningful, purposeful life. Leadership scholar and ethicist Joanne Ciulla (2000) said it beautifully, "work gives people identity, self-worth, and the sense that they can shape and influence the world around them" (p. 21). People desire to contribute to something larger than themselves. According to public health researchers Ozaki et al. (2012), "Psychological wellbeing is predicted by meaningful work." People's mental health and overall sense of wellbeing is affected by organizational participation. In their study of 1,137 people, Ozaki et al. (2012) explored the relationship of contribution to society and workplace psychological distress finding that to the degree people associate their work with contribution to society at large, people experience increased wellbeing.

Contribution, as we define it, refers to the degree by which people are aware of, have clarity around, and are committed to organizational mission, vision, and long-term goals including seeing directly how what they do (job role) contributes. In some respects, contribution is a person's perceived sense of personal influence, power, and capacity to make decisions. People need to have a sense of agency, that sense that they can, within their sphere of influence, make decisions or have input contributing to organizational objectives. The degree that a person feels their work is contributing to the whole is related to a person's sense of community.

Community

People have a distinct need to be an individual and to also identify with and belong within a group. Clinical psychologists McMillan and Chavis (1986) proposed the following criteria in their definition of sense of community, "a feeling that members have of belonging, a feeling that members matter to one another and to the group, and a shared faith that members' needs will be met through their commitment to be together." A person's feeling of belonging amidst a number of relational connections reinforces a sense of social cohesion or solidarity one feels with the group. For example, how one feels with their family is often strongly cohesive because there is long history, strong emotional connection, and a sense of being part of the family. The phrase *blood is thicker than water* refers to that sense of cohesion felt among family members. So too among groups, people can feel a strong sense of bonding resultant from working together. In their exploration of the relationship between sense of community and psychological empowerment, Ramos-Vidal et al. (2020) found a "strong association between personal psychological sense of community and psychological empowerment."

Interpersonal relationships and a person's sense of community positively translates to a person's empowerment, the power and agency a person feels that they must accomplish something. The importance of this connection is the way a person's sense of psychological empowerment was found to be contributory to "higher levels of work satisfaction, organizational commitment, and job performance" (Liden et al., 2000). One's sense of belonging influences one's belief that their contributions matter, increasing their overall commitment to the organization.

Group choice; access to one another formally and informally; visible symbols, celebration of ceremonies, holidays, and significant memories represent powerful ways to mark and commemorate shared history; therein, increasing shared emotional connections. Increased opportunities to interact creates an increased likelihood that people will become close (McMillan & Chavis, 1986; Wenger, 1998), enhancing opportunities for formal and informal collaboration.

Collaboration

Collaboration was defined by consulting scientist Mattessich et al. (2001) as "a mutually beneficial and well-defined relationship entered into by two or more [people, departments, or organizations] to achieve common goals" (p. 4). Many different voices and points of view are exchanged and encouraged through various encounters, exchanges, and perhaps even clashes. Sawyer (2017) described an iron sharpening iron approach where people build on other's ideas. Collaboration, particularly during imagining something new, may resemble an improvisation.

People's capacity to collaborate is influenced in part by the degree of group autonomy, independence, and decision making permitted within the organization, which communicates freedom of thought and action. Sawyer (2007) expressed these as tensions related to (a) a critical analytical mind versus out of box mind, (b) centralized control versus emergent groups, and (c) order and control versus improvisation which is more uncontrollable. High levels of freedom imply more perceived autonomy and opportunity for individual discretion and decision making. One's experience of freedom may be influenced by shared norms about appropriate forms of knowledge; organizational structure, degree of hierarchy and degree of control (e.g., centralized versus emergent) and order and control via formal policies, informal policies, rules, and protocols. Organizations tout creativity and innovation as essential and tend to think in terms of what it would look like to have a collaborative organization characterized as creative and innovative.

Creativity

Creativity was defined by Amabile (1988) as "the production of novel and useful ideas by an individual or small group" and innovation as the "successful implementation of creative ideas within an organization." This definition points to group work and collaboration as important to people's capacity to be creative. Others seem to agree, for example, Sawyer (2007) in his book *Group Genius* asserted that "collaboration is the secret to breakthrough creativity" (p. ix), and Farrell (2001) explored the way collaborative circle's function, including their influence on creativity.

When exploring climate as an organizational metaphor, Ekvall (1987) noted: "Climate affects organizational and psychological processes such as communication, problem solving, decision making, conflict handling, learning and motivation . . . The individual is affected by the climate as a whole, by the general psychological atmosphere." Expanding on this, *creative climate* research explored how individual perceptions activate creativity and innovation within organizations (Ekvall, 1996, 1997, 1987; Ekvall & Ryhammar, 1998, 1999; Hunter et al., 2007). *Idea time*, a term coined by Hunter et al. (2007), referred to the amount of time afforded to and used by people to explore new ideas or creative practices. When idea time is high, people can explore and develop new ideas that were not included in the original mission, vision, or goal. Idea time suggests that creativity and innovation emerge over time, so it is important to allow time and space for incubation and emergence of new ideas (Sawyer, 2007). The way new ideas are received and the environment, including the architecture, within which new ideas may be presented represents *idea support*. In a high idea support environment, people receive ideas and suggestions attentively and professionally and listen to one another. On another level, leadership style and organizational resources such as collaborative space and access to information, are supportive of and available to facilitate, encourage, and to implement creative ideas.

Communication

Communication is instrumental to creating high trust and open contexts where people feel more comfortable taking risks, sharing ideas, and being frank and honest. Clear, honest, and effective communication is essential to building relationships and creating an environment wherein a person feels they can talk openly. Effective communication contributes to a perceived sense of togetherness and psychological safety contributing to social cohesion. This is consistent with Sawyer's (2007) observations about how familiarity, shared tacit knowledge, and shared conventions positively contribute to group cohesion and psychological safety. Additionally, people pay attention to and assign importance or priority to the things talked about by leaders. The expression, *he talks out of both sides of his mouth* refers to the belief that a person's words and deeds are out of sync. Open honest communication within an organization contributes a great deal to the overall organizational climate.

Consultant and speaker Margaret Wheatley's (2005) four stages of solving complex problems, each with specific spatial orientations, is useful when considering how the physical environment affects communication.

1. The circle represents cooling and quieting, a calming of the mind sufficiently to listen to and hear other voices within the group. The circle is proposed as a form contributing to peacefulness and a sense of wholeness and interconnectedness. The circle is an egalitarian shape – no head or sides. Circles, said Wheatley (2005), "create soothing space, where even reticent people can realize that their voice is welcome."
2. Square spaces are helpful in highlighting the complexity of a situation by revealing different perspectives and points of views. A square is used to afford people an opportunity to choose a side. If you begin with a square, prior to a circle, people will have already entrenched toward a position; therefore, it is important to start with a circle so that all voices are heard.
3. A half circle is used to deepen individual and group understanding about the nature of a problem. Use white boards, flip charts, or other forms of spaces within which people can draw, brainstorm, and learn more about the situation being discussed.
4. Use a triangular shape when you need a group to get to work, act, make tough decisions. The triangle symbolically and physically directs attention toward the problem.

Context

When assessing organizational identity and effectiveness, we understand that context matters. Context is, in part, a communication of who an organization is and what is valued. Context is a multidimensional aspect for an organization to consider including such factors as state or regional culture and governance, the physical environment; regulatory environment; customers; sector (e.g., retail, manufacturing, public etc.) and other aspects of culture.

One of the aspects of context is how architecture feels within a space. Day (2014) described buildings as being ensouled where there is the visual context (e.g., the building in relation to a skyline or line of sight) and then there is how a building contributes to the "street atmosphere." Architecture can be perceived as beautiful, fitting, and even hospitable which translates into how an organization is perceived. Material factors such as architecture, interior design, and decor communicate values and create a sense of welcome. On another level, the physical representation of an organization communicates how it values the environment, including nature.

These six human values can be translated into 21 architectural values supportive of an organization's capacity to meet their human value commitments.

Understanding an organization's identity, culture, climate, and structure, its values, and how human values and architectural values are currently demonstrated, lays a foundation from which Use Strategies may be articulated.

Use Strategies

Architectural values connect to an organization's commitment to human values governing an organization's sense of direction and decision making regarding its built environment. Although the nature of leadership has changed, Redman (2017) noted, "In a more complex unpredictable and connected world . . . one aspect of the workplace has remained stubbornly consistent – the spaces that leaders work in." She echoed Steelcase (2016) research indicating that although the demands placed on leaders have changed, their physical offices and overall workplace has remained the same. This observation led Steelcase (2016) to question, "whether leaders have considered the possibility that their workspace could be a catalyst" for the types of changes and behaviors they are striving to enact. Steelcase further asserted, "The physical workplace is an important agent within an organization that can enable openness, transparency and flexibility, helping leaders create the conditions for an engaged, agile and resilient workforce." Architecture informs context and ultimately informs leadership and human endeavors in many ways.

Use Strategies amplify human and architectural values and can be used in thinking about physical design. We have talked about the three legs of our proposed triangle being dialogical and interdependent. Building Elements define physical habitation, Design Principles shapes our overall experience and Use Strategies are those strategies overtly influencing humans' translation of space to place, therein contributing to human flourishing.

Our built environment interacts with our heart and our being in ways both tangible and intangible. Day (2014) overtly declared that "environmental design unavoidably affects the spirit, hence our outlook, values and actions" (p. 6). The built environment directly influences a person's lived experiences within a space. Architecture's overall design communicates values and supports five categories of Use Strategies related to human performance: instrumental, physical, wellbeing (individual and group), social/symbolic, esthetic/spiritual, and spatial.

Instrumental

Instrumentality questions what activities are necessary, how people will use the space, and the functions necessary to support organizational mission and goals. In some respects, this category is closely aligned with Building Elements. Researchers Chan et al. (2007) suggested that by attending to the instrumental design we simultaneously support work processes, people's preferences and needs, and organizational objectives and aims. For example, an office space typically includes access/egress, desks, production space, conference space, break room, and a rest room. Physical space design considers those features necessary to support performance factors such as production, efficiency, and quality related to accomplishing organizational mission and goals.

Instrumentality explores how the built environment facilitates work accomplishment including group interaction, problem solving, decision making, contribution, collaboration, and creativity. Another consideration is the accessibility of physical, social, and information resources to support decision making (Elsbach & Bechky, 2007). In laterally organized groups, instrumental design should consider how the physical space aids collaboration. For example, multidisciplinary project teams needing to review construction drawings and documents may need a large space where materials are co-located. Walls and closed doors are powerful signifiers relative to privacy, openness, and boundaries versus open configurable spaces where people can gather in an ad hoc way. Flexible configurable spaces contribute to co-location of expertise, enhancing communication, information transfer, and problem solving (Elsbach & Bechky, 2007).

Features include:

* Adaptable, configurable, and functional spaces to aid individual and group problem solving, communication, and decision making.
* Access to others, data, and social resources to facilitate collaboration by navigating access, privacy, and intergroup communication.

Physical Requirements

Designing a built environment considers health and wellbeing, ergonomics, process safety, and overall security. Within the United States, the Williams-Steiger Occupational Safety and Health Act of 1970 requires, in part, that employers covered under the Act furnish employees a place of employment free from recognized hazards that are causing or are likely to cause death or serious physical harm to employees.

The U.S. Department of Labor Occupational Safety and Health Administration (OSHA, About, n.d.) was created to ensure safe and healthful working conditions for workers. Use of the phrases *sick-building syndrome* [and *building related illnesses*] physically connected health to physical space including such symptoms as: eye irritation, throat irritation, headaches, fatigue, lack of concentration, shortness of breath, cough, wheeze, rash, dryness, abnormal odor perception, or visual disturbances (Redlich et al., 1997). Factors potentially contributive to human sickness in workplaces include: chemical, biological, ventilation, electromagnetic radiation, freshness of ambient air, psychological factors, and poor and inappropriate lighting (Joshi, 2008). Fortunately, buildings can be designed to mitigate the potential for sick building syndrome (cf. OSHA Technical Manual Section III, Chapter 2).

The field of ergonomics is designed to protect people from risks such as "lifting heavy items, bending, reaching overhead, pushing and pulling heavy loads, working in awkward body postures and performing the same or similar tasks repetitively" (OSHA, Ergonomics, n.d.). Design considerations include such factors as injury resistant design; ergonomically sound designs (e.g., chairs, desk height, etc.); physical comfort (e.g., noise, temperature, or sensory factors such as smell, textures); and nontoxic/nonpathogenic environments. Cognitive ergonomic factors consider the effect of physical space on mental processes such as perception, memory, and reasoning. For example, long-term computer use in a low-lit area with a poorly suited chair can contribute to cognitive fatigue.

Some organizations may have an increased risk and necessity to consider physical personal protection due to heavy equipment usage, confined spaces, high voltage, onsite chemicals, etc. Additionally, physical protection systems related to operational risk, resilience, and vulnerability include due consideration for physical, operational, technology, and personnel monitoring and protection. For example, due to increased concerns related to active shooter preparedness, organizations increase physical security and access features (e.g., locks, barriers, controlled access, cameras, etc.) to protect the organization.

Features include:

- Efficient air quality, ventilation, and air flow and select and use materials of construction specifically selected to reduce contaminants and to ensure an adequate supply of fresh outdoor air through natural or mechanical ventilation.

- Individual selection of personal "tools" such as desk, chair, lighting, headsets, or other necessary tools.
- People have a voice into design and control over amount of light, sound, and temperature (Stokols, 1992; Vischer, 2008) and their preferences contributing to physiological satisfaction, well-being, happiness, and sense of security.
- Access to the outdoors or a gym where a person can take care of their physical body.
- Physical protection features including security, monitoring, and signage.

Social/Symbolic

Humans translate space into place, becoming identified as part of the place in a meaningful way. If the organizational structure arranges people into groups, the physical design reinforces this arrangement. Experiences of the social and symbolic shape individual and group identity, sense of community, and belonging, further influencing how social networks are constructed and the types of social capital exchanged within the network. Human centered design experts Becker and Sims (2001) suggested:

> Rather than thinking of the office as a place primarily for solitary activity, from which one occasionally breaks out in time and space to settings intended for social activity, the office is designed primarily as a social setting, from which one occasionally seeks out more private places for contemplation, concentration, and confidentiality.

Doors, walls, and access points can serve as demarcation points for individual and group territory experienced as feelings of openness, boundedness, and span of control. The ability to regulate a person's environment including one's access within the environment is important to the way a person experiences the built environment (Chan et al., 2007; Elsbach & Bechky, 2007; Heerwagen et al., 1995; Stokols, 1992).

The built environment affirms individual distinctiveness and personalization influencing the meaning a person ascribes to the organization while simultaneously fostering group identity, cohesion, and collaboration. Having an ability to regulate between the public and private contributes to a person's wellbeing (Heerwagen et al., 1995). Balancing public and private spaces affirm group status and preserves an individual need for privacy, lack of distractions, and agency over access to their person. Individual and group social cohesion is enhanced by providing opportunities for social contact and collaboration which affirm feelings of working together collectively toward a common goal (Heerwagen et al., 1995; Stokols, 1992).

Features include:

- Spaces for individual privacy and group interaction providing planned and spontaneous opportunities for meeting and engaging with people. Include physical, visual, and auditory privacy.
- People either individually or as a group incorporate personal artifacts (e.g., pictures, etc.) and symbols fostering culture, group identity, and a sense of uniqueness.
- Spaces for individual and collective reflection, contemplation, and celebration.
- Café or break room with moveable furniture to facilitate formal or informal gathering around food and beverage.

Esthetic Spiritual

We feel the esthetic and spiritual qualities of a place without perhaps being able to articulate what it is about a place that makes us feel a certain way. Others have noted this seemingly intangible experience related to humans and architecture. For examples, Norwegian architect, author, and academic Norberg-Schulz (1980) used the term *genius loci*, the sense of or spirit of place, to describe the architect's task as being "to create meaningful places, whereby he helps man to dwell." Day (2014) noted "the built environment affects the spirit, influences outlook, sensitivities, and thought mobility . . . few people think about architecture, but many feel it" (pp. 2, 6). Environmental psychology researcher Stokols (1990) described spirituality-oriented approaches which consider the "environment as an end it itself." This viewpoint moves toward understanding the socio-physical environment as a context in which to cultivate desired human values.

Human behavior, sense of wellbeing, and the psyche are affected by the built environment. Physical space becomes place as people feel an emotional connection, a sense of attachment. Elsbach and Bechky (2007) used the phrase *emotional home* to designate feelings people have for their workplace. A space becomes a place through activities, actions, and the associated meaning people ascribe to the place. This tendency toward associating place with those activities serves to reinforce a person's sense of belonging and attachment. Esthetic design considers features such as space, lines, form or shape, patterns, lights, colors, sound, temperature, and textures which contribute psychological and sociocultural meanings, informing the shaping of organizational culture and climate. How a place looks and is experienced is a powerful signifier of an organizational identity.

Features include:

- Line of sight and access to daylight and nature.
- Live plants specifically known to increase air quality.
- Color, shapes, variability of textures, lighting, and decorative elements such as art to create an ambience consistent with the organization identity.
- Visually interesting public areas, hallways, and access points.

Spatial Network

Multisite, geographically dispersed locations and our ubiquitous use of technologies suggests an expansion of our thinking about architecture to the virtual. People's move toward the virtual was further laid bare during the pandemic characterized by stay-at-home and work from home. Sociologist Ray Oldenburg (1999) in his study of space denoted three spheres of human existence: home, work, and settings for informal life. In 2009, Stokols et al. asserted that Oldenburg's schema no longer captures the variety of spaces or places given a person's "virtual life." Virtual spaces inform our identities, influencing communication, sense of belonging, and attachment.

The COVID-19 pandemic introduced new organizational considerations around personnel safety including social distancing, disinfection, restricted movements, and associated signage. As mentioned previously our collective move from work to home, blurred lines including the associations we hold with place as pertinent to each. Via technologies such as Zoom and Microsoft Teams, people were invited into other people's homes. People were simultaneously asynchronous and synchronous, connecting as needed to collaborate, make decisions, and interact.

This turn toward an increasingly technology-mediated-interaction, according to Augé (2008) raises concerns in the way "the individual . . . is decentered from himself [due to technology use] . . . the individual can thus live rather oddly in an intellectual, musical, or visual environment that is wholly independent of his immediate physical surroundings." As noted in the section describing leadership challenges, people can work independently at home and use technology to connect, communicate, and collaborate but there remains a high value in face-to-face interactions to facilitate socialization, learning, collaboration, and vital informal conversations. Lessons learned from Covid-19 are changing the way we imagine work and the physical spaces necessary to support the post-Covid-19 expectations. This increases our understanding of how essential intentional design is for our built environment.

Features include:

- Practical considerations for virtual work include technology (hardware, software, and cyber-security), bandwidth, internet speeds, and availability.
- Flexible physical designs affording responsiveness to social distancing and restricted movement.
- Reconsideration of work and physical design with due consideration to simultaneously asynchronous and synchronous behaviors. Distinctions between collaborative work (at the physical office) to individual work (home)
- Seamless remote collaboration spaces.

The human needs pertinent to instrumental, physical, social/symbolic, esthetic spiritual, and spatial network influence features selected when designing a new space.

Chapter Summary

Organizational identity, culture, climate, and structure reflectively communicate a social architecture in terms of what an organization looks like and how it functions, and a deep understanding of this is vital for organizational self-awareness. The human and architectural values that arise from this awareness can be translated into Use Strategies which affect human wellbeing and flourishing. It truly is at the human level that we learn how an organization works, including how the context supports work performance and people's lived experiences. In the next chapter, we describe five different leaders' perceptions of architecture and leadership.

References

Amabile, T. M. (1988). A model of creativity and innovation in organizations. *Research in Organizational Behavior, 10,* 123–167.

Augé, M. (2008). *Non-places: Introduction to an anthropology of supermodernity.* Verso.

Barbera, K. M., & Schneider, B. (2014). *The Oxford handbook of organizational climate and culture.* Oxford University Press.

Beard, A., & Fayard, A. (2021, March 16). Workplace design, post-pandemic (Back to Work, Better). HBR Ideacast Vol. 784. *Harvard Business Review.* https://hbr. org/podcast/2021/03/workplace-design-post-pandemic

Becker, F., & Sims, W. (2001). *Offices that work: Balancing communication, flexibility, and cost* (International Workplace Studies Program). Cornell University. www. interruptions.net/literature/Becker_Sims-Offices_That_Work-IWS_0002.pdf

Bolman, L. G., & Deal, T. E. (2013). *Reframing organizations: Artistry, choice, and leadership* (5th ed.). Jossey-Bass.

Chan, J. K., Beckman, S. L., & Lawrence, P. G. (2007). Workplace design: A new managerial imperative. *California Management Review*, *49*(2), 6–22. https://doi.org/10.2307/41166380

Ciulla, J. B. (2000). *The working life: The promise and betrayal of modern work.* Times Books.

Congdon, C., Flynn, D., & Redman, M. (2014). Balancing "We" and "Me": The best collaborative spaces also support solitude. *Harvard Business Review*, 50–57.

Cruikshank, J. L., & Malcolm, C. (1994). *Herman Miller, Inc.: Buildings and beliefs.* The American Institute of Architects Press.

Day, C. (2014). *Places of the soul: Architecture and environmental design as healing art* (3rd ed.). Routledge.

Ekvall, G. (1987). The climate metaphor in organizational theory. In B. M. Bass, & S. D. Drenth (Eds.), *Advances in organizational psychology* (pp. 177–190). Sage.

Ekvall, G. (1996). Organizational climate for creativity and innovation. *European Journal of Work and Organizational Psychology*, *5*(1), 105–123. https://doi.org/10.1080/13594329608414845

Ekvall, G. (1997). Organizational conditions and levels of creativity. *Creativity and Innovation Management*, *6*(4), 195–205. https://doi.org/10.1111/1467-8691.00070

Ekvall, G., & Ryhammar, L. (1998). Leadership style, social climate and organizational outcomes: A study of a Swedish university college. *Creativity and Innovation Management*, *7*(3), 126–130. https://doi.org/10.1111/1467-8691.00100

Ekvall, G., & Ryhammar, L. (1999). The creative climate: Its determinant and effects at a Swedish university. *Creativity Research Journal*, *12*(4), 303–310. https://doi.org/10.1207/s15326934crj1204_8

Elsbach, K. D., & Bechky, B. A. (2007). It's more than a desk: Working smarter through leveraged office design. *California Management Review*, *49*(2), 80–101. https://doi.org/10.2307/41166384

Farrell, M. P. (2001). *Collaborative circles: Friendship dynamics & creative work.* University of Chicago Press.

Fayard, A.-L., Weeks, J., & Khan, M. (2021, March 1). Designing the Hybrid office. *Harvard Business Review*. https://hbr.org/2021/03/designing-the-hybrid-office

Hatch, M. J., & Schultz, M. (2002). The dynamics of organizational identity. *Human Relations*, *55*(8), 989–1018. https://doi.org/10.1177/0018726702055008181

Heerwagen, J. H., Heubach, J. G., Montgomery, J., & Weimer, W. C. (1995). Environmental design, work, and well being: Managing occupational stress through changes in the workplace environment. *AAOHN Journal*, *43*(9), 458–468. https://doi.org/10.1177/216507999504300904

Hunter, S. T., Bedell, K. E., & Mumford, M. D. (2007). Climate for creativity: A quantitative review. *Creativity Research Journal*, *19*(1), 69–90. https://doi.org/10.1080/10400410709336883

Joshi, S. M. (2008). The sick building syndrome. *Indian Journal of Occupational Environmental Medicine*, *12*(2), 61–64. https://doi.org/10.4103/0019-5278.43262

Liden, R. C., Wayne, S. J., & Sparrowe, R. T. (2000). An examination of the mediating role of psychological empowerment on the relations between the job, interpersonal relationships, and work outcomes. *Journal of Applied Psychology*, *85*(3), 407–416. https://doi.org/10.1037/0021-9010.85.3.407

Mattessich, P. W., Murray-Close, M., Monsey, B. R., & Foundation, A. H. W. (2001). *Collaboration: What makes it work* (2nd ed.). Amherst H. Wilder Foundation.

McMillan, D. W., & Chavis, D. M. (1986). Sense of community: A definition and theory. *Journal of Community Psychology*, *14*(1), 6–23. https://doi.org/10.1002/1520-6629(198601)14:1<6::AID-JCOP2290140103>3.0.CO;2-I

Morrell, P., Langdon, R., Marmot, A., Steevens, J., Ellis, R., McVean, B., & Selby, I. (2006). *The impact of office design on business performance.* Commission for Architecture & The Built Environment and the British Council for Offices. www.designcouncil.org.uk/resources/report/impact-office-design-business-performance

Norberg-Schulz, C. (1980). *Genius loci: Towards a phenomenology of architecture.* Rizzoli.

Occupational Safety and Health Administration (OSHA). (n.d.). *About.* www.osha.gov/aboutosha#:~:text=OSHA's%20Mission,%2C%20outreach%2C%20education%20and%20assistance

Occupational Safety and Health Administration (OSHA). (n.d.). *Ergonomics.* Retrieved from www.osha.gov/ergonomics

Oldenburg, R. (1999). *The great good place: Cafés, coffee shops, bookstores, bars, hair salons, and other hangouts at the heart of a community.* Marlowe.

Ozaki, K., Motohashi, Y., Kaneko, Y., & Fujita, K. (2012). Association between psychological distress and a sense of contribution to society in the workplace. *BMC Public Health*, *12*, 253. https://doi.org/10.1186/1471-2458-12-253. https://bmcpublichealth.biomedcentral.com/track/pdf/10.1186/1471-2458-12-253.pdf

Ramos-Vidal, I., Palacio, J., Uribe, A., Villamil, I., & Castro, B. (2020). Sense of community, psychological empowerment, and relational structure at the individual and organizational levels: Evidence from a multicase study. *Journal of Community Psychology*, *48*(2), 398–413. https://doi.org/10.1002/jcop.22261

Redlich, C. A., Sparer, J., & Cullen, M. R. (1997). Sick-building syndrome. *Lancet (London, England)*, *349*(9057), 1013–1016. https://doi.org/10.1016/S0140-6736(96)07220-0

Redman, M. (2017). *Designing spaces for the connected leader.* www.management-issues.com/opinion/7265/designing-spaces-for-the-connected-leader/

Ropo, A., Paoli, D. D., Salovaara, P., & Sauer, E. (2015). Why does space need to be taken seriously in leadership and organization studies and practice? In A. Ropo, P. Salovaara, E. Sauer, & D. De Paoli (Eds.), *Leadership in spaces and places* (pp. 1–23). Edward Elgar.

Sawyer, R. K. (2017). *Group genius: The creative power of collaboration.* Basic Books.

Schein, E. H. (2010). *Organizational culture and leadership* (4th ed., Vol. 2). Jossey-Bass.

Schneider, B., Ehrhart, M. G., & Macey, W. H. (2013). Organizational climate and culture. *The Annual Review of Psychology*, *64*, 361–388. https://doi.org/10.1146/annurev-psych-113011-143809

Slingerland, E. G. (2014). *Trying not to try: The art and science of spontaneity.* Crown.

Steelcase. (2016). The new leader. *360 Magazine*, 71. www.steelcase.com/content/uploads/2016/10/360_Magazine_Issue71.pdf

Stokols, D. (1990). Instrumental and spiritual views of people-environment relations. *American Psychologist*, *45*(5), 641–646. https://doi.org/10.1037/0003-066x.45.5.641

Stokols, D. (1992). Establishing and maintaining healthy environments: Toward a social ecology of health promotion. *American Psychologist, 47*(1), 6–22. https://doi.org/10.1037/0003-066x.47.1.6

Stokols, D., Misra, S., Runnerstrom, M. G., & Hipp, J. A. (2009). Psychology in an age of ecological crisis: From personal angst to collective action. *American Psychologist, 64*(3), 181–193. https://doi.org/10.1037/a0014717

Vischer, J. (2008). Towards an environmental psychology of workspace: How people are affected by environments for work. *Architectural Science Review, 51*(2), 97–108. https://doi.org/10.3763/asre.2008.5114

Wenger, E. (1998). *Communities of practice: Learning, meaning, and identity.* Cambridge University Press.

Wheatley, M. J. (2005). *Finding our way: Leadership for an uncertain time.* Berrett-Koehler.

7 Architecture and Leadership in Action

Introduction

Around 2,000 years ago, the Roman emperor Vespasian made the strategic leadership decision to replace the Golden House of Nero, representative of imperial wealth and privilege, with the Colosseum, a sports palace for the people of Rome. This decision wasn't made because Vespasian had decided that emperors weren't deserving of such splendor, but rather because he had decided that the best way to control and rule the people of Rome was to occupy them with entertainment and food. Therefore, his architecture became a key, strategic part of his overall leadership strategy.

Around 250 years ago, the leaders of the new nation of the United States of America decided to use their architecture very strategically as well. But this time, instead of employing it to control subjects, the architecture was used to extol new kinds of democratic values and culture to the nation and the world. Everything about the United States was new. It was a democracy in a world of monarchies, with an elected president in a world of kings, where people had rights and responsibilities of citizens. The United States needed an architecture to communicate all these democratic values.

The genius of Pierre L'Enfant, the designer of Washington DC, was to take recognizable and respected monarchical forms and translate them to reflect democratic ideals. He envisioned a grand capital of wide avenues, public squares, and inspiring buildings arranged around a centerpiece of a great public space, which would be the people's domain. As opposed to dedicating the grandest spot for the leader's palace, he placed Congress at the highest point with a commanding view. Capitol Hill became the center of the design, from which everything radiated. Thus, the architecture of Washington D.C. is symbolic of the values and aspirations of democracy to the world.

Put forth thus far is the assertion that if applied thoughtfully and cohesively, architecture and leadership can work together to powerfully

DOI: 10.4324/9781003166788-7

influence organizational identity, culture, climate, and structure. Specifically, architecture can and should be an essential component of leadership strategy. Throughout, we've shown examples of buildings exemplifying the power and potential of the Critical Components of Architecture: Building Elements, Design Principles, and Use Strategies. The following case studies and conversations with successful, contemporary leaders now provide an opportunity to consider what this multifaceted approach looks like in today's ever-changing world. Specifically, five organizational leaders were interviewed to learn (a) Ways they employ the built environment as a shaper of their context, organizational identity, culture, climate, and structure; (b) How their built environment communicates values; and (c) Why architecture is important and useful to leadership.

Those interviewed included: the Dougherty Art Center, an art center in Austin, Texas; Esri, a pioneer in geospatial location services and software in Redlands, California; Gensler, the world's largest architecture firm; Siemens Healthineers, a multinational, high-tech conglomerate; and St. Ignatius Chapel, a chapel at a Catholic university in Seattle, Washington. We believe these five examples affirm the importance of human and architectural values articulated to support function and experience. The purpose of this chapter is to present the stories of the leaders interviewed, followed by an analysis and discussion of lessons learned. Direct quotations from those interviewed are italicized.

Dougherty Art Center: Austin's Cultural Living Room

The Dougherty Arts Center has been a presence in Austin, Texas, since 1978 as a home for both emerging and established artists to create and experience art firsthand. Part of their mission is to be *Austin's cultural living room* where all people are welcome to gather and create community. The Dougherty Arts Center (DAC) currently offers three experiences: The Dougherty Theater, Julia C. Butridge Gallery, and the Dougherty Arts School. The City of Austin Parks and Recreation Department (PARD) is in the process of moving the DAC out of the former Navy and Marine Reserve Center, originally built in 1947, to nearby Zilker Park, Austin's central park, and the hub of numerous cultural attractions.

PARD is in the design phase of a multifaceted process to design and replace the DAC. PARD's Client Representative, Laura Esparza, Division Manager for Museums and Cultural Programs, described how following a 2010 conditions assessment determining that the current building was beyond its viability, PARD began a feasibility and community engagement process. This process included site studies, envisioning the new space, hosting a series of community open houses, and presenting outcomes to the City of Austin Boards, Commission, and City Council. From these efforts, a number of functional requirements and human values rose to the top (PARD, 2019):

- Public gathering areas (inside and outside) that foster a sense of community.
- Spaces that inspire creativity.
- Gallery space meeting the requirements of the Smithsonian Institution (PARD holds an Affiliation with the Smithsonian).
- Rentable rehearsal rooms and public spaces that can be reserved by students, faculty, or the public.
- New technology options for students and faculty.
- Spaces flexible enough to serve multiple needs, yet able to accommodate their specific function well.
- Facility that embraces the history and emotion of the DAC.
- Top words to describe the new DAC facility: flexible, cutting edge, light, functional, industrial, human scale, comfortable, and beautiful.
- 100% of respondents said a connection to nature is important to consider.

These functional requirements and human values were translated into three preliminary design alternatives presented to the community through a series of public engagements. After the community engagement process, the preliminary design alternatives were presented to the City of Austin Boards, Commissions, and City Council.

San Antonio's Overland Partners was selected as the architect to design a new DAC (Figure 7.1), aided by charge architects Studio 8. According to

Figure 7.1 Architect's illustration of the exterior of the Dougherty Arts Center, Austin Texas. Image courtesy of Overland Partners Architects.

Overland Partners (Overland Partners, Culture and Practice, n.d.), their focus is the creation of "human-centered architecture," using a "rigorous, collaborative process" "Unlocking the Embedded Potential™ of [client's] vision to create places that care for the earth, promote well-being, and lead to measurable human transformation." Talking about their design process, Overland noted, "We know good design doesn't happen by accident. It is intentional." Overland's trademarked process, The Human Handprint™ includes specific impacts desired for each project, including:

1. Aspiration – why of the project.
2. Inspiration – elevate the human experience.
3. Relationships – align the natural environment with people.
4. Stewardship – environmental, operational and financial resources.
5. Well-being – strategies that support both physical and mental health.

These values intersect in meaningful ways with PARD's values and vision for the new DAC.

Ms. Esparza remarked about the design process, *I think we got everything we wanted.* This was no small feat given the vision, values, and desired functionality for the envisioned facility. This project is an example of how much can be accomplished through careful, intentional design. Overland's *Human Handprint* process was specifically mentioned as a process that allowed the designers to empathetically hear and respond to the mission, values, and culture envisioned for the DAC. This resulted in a design that, from an artist's perspective, makes them feel that the architecture works with them and for them, and *is on their side.*

When talking with artists and current staff about the new facility, Ms. Esparza poignantly remarked that when she shows artists and staff the plans, *they cry tears of joy.* Those who experienced the current facility understand the significance and the rarity presented by an opportunity to create a new design that meets the vision and values desired by the community, a vision translating their mission, work, culture, and the needs of their desired target audiences. As they've progressed through the various phases of vision and design, Ms. Esparza and the DAC staff fully see and feel the pressure of this as a once in a lifetime opportunity. Ms. Esparza remarked, *you don't get many shots [like this].* They want to get it right and clearly see the importance of the process, being intentional about design decisions, making sure the functional, esthetic, and experiential design integrates with nature and the space within which the building is situated.

The DAC will embody the vision to be *Austin's Cultural Living Room* by being open, welcoming, fluid, transparent, and connected to the land.

Embracing the four directions, pathways connect the building to the natural environment making it a *place for all arts for all people*. The proposed DAC welcomes and acknowledges the Native Americans who historically lived on the site near the river by connecting meaningfully to the land and the majestic, historic oak trees on the site. An important aspect of the design is to symbolically consecrate the land, making it sacred for the past, present, and future. The relationship to the surrounding trees is visual and material, as the core of the building will be brick, symbolically echoing tree trunk solidity and texture. The upper part of the building will be wrapped in a metal screen to reflect the porosity and light effects of tree foliage.

Artists, gathered and consulted by the DAC's design team, desired a building that would inspire. One of the ways they saw that being possible was to create a building that would accomplish this idea of outside-in and inside-out with the exterior resulting from the interior, which is both reflective of a Native American concept, and a theater arts approach familiar to Ms. Esparza. The inner spaces of Overland's design are for making, while being inspired by the nature outside, and the exterior courtyard spaces are to function like interior gallery spaces. The interior will include educational spaces, cultural spaces, making spaces, and social spaces. The main mixing space at the intersection of the four directional paths is *The Hive*, which will be a space for mixing the inside and outside, a space buzzing with people.

Social spaces such as The Hive were very important as places with shared amenities such as coffee, food, and art-making materials, to foster conversations, collaboration, and community life. There will be numerous outdoor patios on the ground floor accessed from the outside, and various balconies accessed from the inside. Each of the main nodes will have an adjacent space for meetings and community gathering. This gives the building and people a *place to breathe*.

A specific example of one of the ways the building will reflect the DAC's mission and provide intentional opportunities to build culture is the children's education node. The focus on children's uses increases the functional need to create a secure and private environment. Ms. Esparza described how children's presence created the need to consider a highly secure and observable environment, without the feeling of being restrained or vulnerably exposed. One creative way to ensure children's privacy was by incorporating windows at floor level in a public hallway adjacent to the children's dance studio. A person walking through the passage will see little feet dancing. This provides visible movement, shared activity, and joy, and also allows light into the studio, while simultaneously ensuring children's privacy. Additionally, a rehearsal space overlooking the lobby incorporates translucent glass so that you can see the shadows of actors rehearsing a play inside while maintaining anonymity. Rick Archer, CEO and a founding partner of Overland Partners, said of the project,

> The Dougherty Arts Center (DAC) has been a remarkable client because they understand so well the connection between physical space and human experience, between design and culture. Laura Esparza has provided extraordinary leadership, leveraging DAC's move to a new building not just to meet growing needs, but to inspire transformation. For the Dougherty Arts Center, architecture is an agent to empower the entire community.

Ms. Esparza, who also runs cultural centers for African American, Mexican American, and Asian American communities in Austin, is also working to help create buildings that respond to the unique cultural aspects of each of those groups. She clearly stated her purpose, *we have to design spaces for our communities . . . coming together as a community.* Reflecting on the process, Ms. Esparza noted, *the space has to be very true to our audience, we have to create authentic spaces acknowledging cultural patterns.* Part of this entails understanding *how others feel comfortable in a space* and *what this comfort means in terms of a group's use patterns.*

Ms. Esparza's extensive experience accomplishing buildings for arts and cultural groups fuels her belief in the power of architecture to make these connections. She looks forward to the day the DAC opens its doors, allowing the staff, artists, and the public to finally experience the space, a space intentionally and purposefully situated within a context with specific purposes and meaning. In thinking about the challenges of such a project, Ms. Esparza asserted, *you have to persist and believe that it's going to be built.* In closing, Ms. Esparza spoke to the vision, saying they will *be amazed when they see what an art center can be when everyone involved deeply listens.*

Esri: The Science of Where

Esri is a world leader in geographic information software (GIS), location intelligence, and mapping. When describing their geographic approach, Esri (n.d.) noted, "Hidden patterns, trends, and relationships emerge when you visualize and analyze data on a map," increasing our ability to understand data in real time and beneficially transforming our ability to quickly make decisions, share data, and collaborate. That Esri is in Redlands, California, instead of a technology center like Silicon Valley or Silicon Beach speaks volumes about the uniqueness of this company. Today, Esri has >5,000 employees from >73 countries, serving >300,000 organizations and millions of individual customers with their technology and services.

Esri was founded by Jack and Laura Dangermond in 1969. We sat down with Mr. Dangermond and Chief Technology Officer James McKinney to learn more about Esri's beginnings, values, and the integral way the built environment is critical to the vision. Mr. Dangermond holds an undergraduate degree from California State Polytechnic University at Pomona in landscape architecture and environmental science, a Master of Architecture degree in urban planning from the University of Minnesota, and a Master of Landscape Architecture from Harvard University.

When asked about the location of Esri, Mr. Dangermond reminded us that when they formed the company in 1969, Silicon Valley and Silicon Beach did not exist. While there were opportunities to start the company at Harvard, Berkeley, and in Minnesota, Redlands was their first choice because this is where he grew up working in his family's nursery business. Redlands offers a good quality of life, beautiful geography, and views of the mountains. Beyond Esri's positive identity and brand, location is another strategic attractor of potential recruits. This connection to and commitment to his hometown was a recurring theme throughout our conversation.

Esri's physical campus is a beautiful site filled with landscaping and boulders, contributing to a feeling of being in a forest. While walking on the grounds, you do not feel as though you're at a technology company due to the lush, green, low-rise campus of wood and glass buildings. Mr. Dangermond said, *it's like coming to a park with some buildings hidden.* No building is more than three stories tall, and there seem to be more walking paths, koi ponds, and gardens than buildings. Despite the huge footprint of some of the buildings, the landscaping makes it almost impossible to see one of them in totality or to get a sense of how many buildings there are.

The Esri campus represents the vision of its leaders. Their passion for nature, beauty, and sustainability is clearly evident in both the design of Esri as a company and the interior and external design of the built environment. Mr. Dangermond said, *I still think of myself as a landscape architect; I used natural materials, and wanted it to appear emerged [from the space] rather than placed.* Interior spaces incorporate potted plants, curves, and lines to create a sense of flow and movement, natural materials, glass partitions to enhance transparency, and windows to create long sight lines and exterior views. The site, organizational structure, and ways they interact reflect *our personalities, embracing a natural, organic style* said Mr. Dangermond.

Hidden within this peaceful, calm environment is a company that produces software that affects the globe in many ways. Esri's global aspirations were summed up by Mr. McKinney when he said, *We're here to build software to save the planet.* Mr. Dangermond echoed, *we do this by giving tools so that work gets better.* The company's global vision and how that is translated into Esri's physical site and office buildings are coherent. Mr. Dangermond stated, *space matters – spatial thinking matters deeply. Spatial proximity really matters. The attributes of the space really matter.* This thinking influences the way work is organized within Esri, as Mr. Dangermond believes that *good managers are very clear about how they organize people spatially, it's a management tool, which is not taught in business school. This arranging facilitates communication.* Thinking of operational needs in terms of proximity affects the way people are organized, with the architecture designed to support these needs. Furthermore, Mr. Dangermond asserted that *good design and landscape design make people happier, more relaxed, and helps them interact more effectively.*

The reason that the campus is made up of multiple buildings spread around the property and that none of those buildings are more than three stories tall is that Mr. Dangermond wants people to walk – both between buildings and up and down stairs once inside each building, with the hope that people will typically skip the elevator and take the stairs to access three stories. Beyond the desire for employees to develop healthy lifestyle habits, a commitment to walking also creates opportunities for casual meetings and conversations on the way to and from offices. There are typically seating, breakout areas, and whiteboards at landings to facilitate quick, informal get-togethers and collaboration. These opportunities also exist throughout each building in informal seating areas, small conference rooms, break and coffee areas, balconies, etc.

Mr. Dangermond greatly desires to promote an informal, ad-hoc, casual atmosphere for employees to create, envision, and expand possibilities, while also being able to find brief periods of respite during the day and inspiration from the natural environment. He said,

> This is going to be a beautiful place to work, and I think that's important. And as people work in their homes more, I want them to have a place to come and to remember the experience of being here . . . One of our ideas was, can people's third place [besides home and work] be here on this campus? That is one of the reasons that we invest so much in landscaping, landscape design, and architecture.

McKinney offered:

> It's comforting – it gives you a mental break to leave your office and walk into this place that's calm and you can come and decompress a little bit. People will come here to the café or to have meetings here [who] don't even work here. They don't understand it, but I think if they thought about it, they would really appreciate it.

The architecture of Esri is very transparent, as best exemplified by the Headquarters building, the Café, and the Technical Support and Training Building, the newest addition to the campus and a clear representation of the evolution of Esri's architecture. According to Mr. Dangermond,

> What you have seen from the first building to the last building is an evolutionary process of evolving and improving things as we went along. The later stages of our architecture are expressed in [the Tech] building with naturalistic curves to match the naturalistic landscape. I'm inspired by being in a forest – in natural landscapes.

This latest architectural manifestation of the evolution of Esri's values and culture in the 11,000 square feet, three-story Technical Support and Training Building, represents a clear blurring of inside and out, with spaces and functions that are normally inside being outside and vice versa. The design of this building incorporates clear lines of site all the way through the building, almost making all the spaces seem exterior.

The building is very open, flexible, and transparent. After walking through the building, Mr. McKinney said, "As we toured the new tech support building, we stood on the south side and could see all the way through the building . . . which represents an evolution." Mr. Dangermond added, *more open – more connected.* Architects DLR Group (n.d.) said the building "immerses employees in the landscape." The Tech building is also very simple in its materiality and has developed the idea of stair as social space to a very high level. The values of connection to people and nature (Figure 7.2) are evident in the way employees can see each other and see outside to constantly connect with the beautiful landscape. This constant connection to nature is highly effective in positively affecting our parasympathetic nervous systems, and in creating a calm, positive environment in which to work.

All of this is also seen to beautiful effect in the café, which is basically a glass structure set in an oasis of trees, flowers, water, and large boulders. Mr. Dangermond personally placed almost every boulder on campus. He commented, *I like rocks – I guess you figured that out. They make me feel good.* He wants all his employees to feel good as well. The architecture's transparency not only provides this comforting connection to nature, it also provides a constant visual connection between employees at every level of the company, promoting openness and collaboration, as seen in full effect in the Headquarters building, the Software Development building, and the Technical Support and Training Building. According to Mr. Dangermond, *We started off with very closed-off buildings. But today almost all offices have window access or windows that provide*

Figure 7.2 The Esri Café, Redlands, CA. Photo by Mark A. Roberson.

light – walls with windows in them so that you can have access to natural light. Another example of breaking down barriers and creating connection is evidenced in the auditorium/community room within the Headquarters building, where instead of a stage separated from the seating area, speakers and first-row seats are on the same level, creating intimacy, a sense of access, and closer proximity.

Reuse, repurpose, recycle were communicated by Mr. Dangermond as vital and as evidenced on Esri's campus. Instead of tearing down old buildings to make room for new, Mr. Dangermond's philosophy is to renovate, add on, or even move and repurpose buildings to make room for new elements. This idea of repurposing is consistent with Mr. Dangermond's view of employees, in which he desires to keep people long-term, focused on personal growth, restoration, and finding new ways for each person to be useful as they grow in the company.

Mr. Dangermond's commitment to Esri and his home of Redlands communicates the idea of an organization that is a good citizen, and a good neighbor. Attracting a rail line, repurposing old buildings, and creating community programming on site with experts on a wide variety of topics, all contribute to Mr. Dangermond's vision and strategy. He said,

We're doing this to make Redlands a more beautiful place so that it attracts the so-called Silicon Valley types so that they have a more interesting life. By revitalizing downtown we've made a lot of things come to life . . . We're fixing up our town so that the campus gets extended into the town through design elements and the town gets connected back to the campus.

Both Mr. Dangermond and Mr. McKinney communicated an even larger vision to connect employee's families and the community to the Esri family. The linkage between thinking geospatially to one's values about work and the natural and built environment interestingly translates into a global leadership perspective. When we asked Mr. Dangermond three things, he'd like other leaders to know, he paused for a moment and then offered:

- Be conscious of what's going on in the world. Understanding precedes action. With understanding how our world is connected, people will act better. The great challenge of our time is understanding and ability to collaborate.
- Have hope. We can do something. We can work. We can bring the human spirit together.
- Think about how you bring about transformational change. Think holistically, think in an integrated way, be sensitive to communities, and care for the environment.

These values are apparent in the intention and attention paid to design, nature, human needs, and the way the company conducts itself in terms of human, customer, community, and environmental relations.

Finally, we asked Mr. Dangermond why so few organizational leaders seem as intentional as he is regarding architecture, landscape, and design. He replied:

Why don't more managers consider spatial thinking? I think it's because they don't have experience in building long-term asset values for their people. If you don't have experience with the fact that space and aesthetics matters, you don't pay attention. And when people understand more, they act better.

We believe Mr. Dangermond is right, and his words are a beautiful summation of why we felt the need to write this book on architecture and leadership.

Gensler: Creating a Better World Through the Power of Design

Gensler is the largest architecture and design firm in the world, and they are engaged in work around the world. With Diane Hoskins, Andy Cohen has served as co-CEO of Gensler since 2005 and was described on the Gensler (n.d.) website as "a champion of the power of design to enhance and enrich the human experience." Andy's perspective is particularly interesting in that Gensler not only has 6,800 employees spread across 52 offices worldwide, they also design all of their own offices as well as those of numerous other organizations of various types and sizes in over 120 countries across the globe. In so doing, Gensler has thought about the intersection of architecture and leadership as both client and designer. Mr. Cohen had many insights on the effects of the architecture they have designed, including useful thoughts on how the many leaders Gensler deals with think about their architecture.

Mr. Cohen, reflecting on his experience, observed a broad evolution in the way many leaders view their built environments due to the ways the Covid 19 pandemic changed how people work and how they view their physical workplaces. Prior to the Covid 19 induced interruption in work patterns, space was often viewed in terms of process efficiency, effectiveness, and workflow, or as an iconic esthetic statement. However, lessons learned from experiences related to remote working, reintegration into the office, and the new normal of office operations, brought the ability of the built environment to encourage participation and connection, to increase confidence in the organization, and to raise esprit de corps, into much more of a focus.

Mr. Cohen (2022), in a Forbes Business Council article, noted, "I believe offices must offer twice the experience they did before the onset of the pandemic. The new office must be an experience multiplier . . . for workers who crave authentic engagement and interaction." Future projects of all types will need to respond to "the new way that people work and live and that reflect the most influential issues we're facing today in climate change, inclusion, and community" (Gensler Research Institute, 2022). For example, in the 2022 edition of the firm's annual "Design Forecast" publication, design leaders state that in education, "students look to schools not just as places of learning – but as places to feel safe, engaged, and included." In other words, the places where people spend their lives and engage in their life's calling must communicate and support human values more effectively than ever before. Cohen (2022) concluded:

> In the post-pandemic future, the office should be a place that motivates workers and supports them in doing their best work. By designing the workplace to serve as an experience multiplier, companies can provide much more than the backdrop for conducting business, making the office a space where creativity, collaboration and innovation thrive.

A leader's ability to flex, adapt, and reimagine work creates new opportunities to meet human values. A mantra that Gensler uses, said Mr. Cohen, is to design offices and workplaces that are *a destination and not an obligation.* This thinking positions architecture as a vital component of leadership, particularly moving forward.

Office designs for Gensler employees and operations emulate Gensler's mission and values. Mr. Cohen said *it's important to stay true to our mission, which is to create a better world through the power of design.* Important elements of that mission, which become apparent in the physical design of Gensler's offices, are collaborative leadership, the ability to listen and respond, care for community, and the scale and the technological capabilities of the firm. For example, it's very important for Gensler's offices to be on the ground floor of their buildings, not hidden away in an office tower. The reason is to facilitate a grounding in, investment in, and connection to the cities and communities in which an office exists. The fact that Gensler has 52 offices around the globe is expressive of the desire to be embedded into each of the communities in which they work as opposed to working out of a single, huge, central office.

This connectedness is exemplified in the Los Angeles office, where the main entrance, communal spaces, and central atrium are on the ground floor, embedded within the community of Downtown Los Angeles. The atrium is designed as a public meeting place – a sort of new town square. This central space serves as a venue for both internal gatherings and external, community-focused events, even hosting the mayor of the city and the governor of California. It puts the office in conversation with its context and also helps influence and shape the design approach of Gensler's architects to pursue the same community embedding strategy in the built environments they design for others.

The spirit of collaboration is physically evident in Gensler's LA office and communicates to visiting clients that Gensler is open to listen and respond to their ideas and needs. Design in this sense is not pre-determined, but instead responsive to a client's vision, mission, identity, and culture. This philosophy is expressed on Gensler's (Services, n.d.) website as "successful buildings capture the spirit of their surroundings, even as they assert their own identity."

The LA office features several conference rooms that are not only very transparent from the central atrium, but which also open onto and, at times, cantilever into that central atrium space. The ground floor also opens to an integrated amphitheater-style seating area in the rear that faces out onto the public plaza and city beyond. This arrangement reinforces the company mantra to design *from the inside out.* The scale of the central atrium and

Figure 7.3 The ground floor atrium space of the Gensler L.A. office, From @ assassiproductions.

the views it affords into the multiple levels and operations of the organization also reinforces the scale of effort that Gensler can bring to bear for a client, one of its great competitive advantages. The main atrium space also communicates the technological capabilities of Gensler to clients and employees alike.

As architects and as a very large company, Gensler is in the business of helping their clients embrace the communicative and symbolic power of architecture. They are employing this philosophy in their own offices in these very specific ways to communicate their organizational values and culture through their architecture. When asked about the intersection of architecture and leadership, Mr. Cohen asserted, *design is the difference maker, and through design, we can make a profound impact on this radically changing world.*

Siemens Healthineers: Breakthroughs in Healthcare. For Everyone. Everywhere

Siemens Healthineers (Purpose, n.d.) is focused on "bringing breakthrough innovations to market, [to] help healthcare professionals to deliver high-quality care, leading to the best possible outcome for patients." In their real estate portfolio, they currently hold >150 locations in the United States, including Research and Design centers, manufacturing sites, and sales and service operations. Dean Lee serves as Head of Asset Management at Siemens Healthineers and is an architect trained at the University of Notre Dame. Being a leader of a major division of a giant corporation and an architect gives Dean a unique view of the possibilities and power of architecture to affect organizational identity, culture, climate, and structure.

Siemens Healthineers' architecture seeks to balance large-scale, advanced technology with human experience, interaction, and care. Mr. Lee said, *this means that their approach to architecture is not about what is most expeditious or even most efficient.* Instead, when considering new or redesign approaches to architecture, they take the time, spend the money, and invest the care into creating high-tech places meaningful to the people using them, exploring every facet from the site selection, to materials, color, and furniture selection. Mr. Lee described shifts in architecture from traditionally arranged (e.g., private offices, conference rooms) to more collaborative-focused communities.

Internally, Siemens Healthineers has established design standards (i.e., the Design Book) and approaches to architecture descriptive of the *Healthineers Way of Working*. The Design Book translates espoused values into enacted values, prescriptively incorporated into the design of Healthineers spaces. Their design begins with forming a multidisciplinary approach (e.g., real estate team, human resources, and information technology) to ensure broad participation and diverse perspectives.

Over the years, Mr. Lee has observed a shift in the focus of their company and their built environments away from being focused on the individual, and toward being focused on the collective and the community. Healthineers' identity and values include such qualities as ownership, pride, care, quality, welcome, good food (bistros), innovation, and sustainability. For example, offices and facilities don't have private offices, even for the CEO and top administration. Instead, each building utilizes a neighborhood design featuring various environments such as private "think tanks," mother's rooms, meditation rooms, etc. Employees use an automated reservation system to reserve a space for working, meeting, or for needed quiet time. Site selection includes selecting spaces near a park, walking trail, pond, etc., to encourage access to nature and physical fitness. This emphasis on physical well-being includes on-site gyms so that employees can exercise physically and socially. An example of honoring employees is an honor wall that shows gratitude to service members in a prominent place. An underlying design principle is to design using the language of *we versus I*, which actively changes the ways they approach the design of their physical environments.

Responding to Covid-19, Mr. Lee acknowledged how people got used to working at home. Covid-19 further shifted their work approach to a schedule of 3 days at the office and Monday and Friday at home to accommodate people's renewed ways of working. Healthineers are also spending millions to change facilities from gas to electric and exploring other sustainable efforts to transform their stated values around sustainability into the built environment. This shift is not solely a reaction to the Covid-19 pandemic but part of a more significant cultural shift at Siemens. The new way of working resultant from the pandemic, however, sped up the transition. Employees learned to do their private, focused work at home, allowing the office to become a more collaborative, collective, and open place.

These physical manifestations of the Healthineers' identity, values, and culture are necessary due to their belief in leading by example, open communication, and being good corporate citizens. Under the guidance of Dean Lee and others, the company is taking every opportunity to use architecture wisely to embody and promote these values, not only as a brand identifier, but as a way to powerfully and materially affect the lives of the people who work for and interact with them.

Figure 7.4 Interior of the Siemens Life Sciences Manufacturing Facility for Corindus, at 275 Grove Street, Newton, MA. Photo courtesy of Alexandria Real Estate Equities, Inc.

St. Ignatius: Gathering of Different Lights

We began this book with a story of a church that missed a major opportunity to use its architecture in a way that would contribute to its mission and values. Our last case study is of a church that took advantage of its unique opportunity beautifully and meaningfully. The Chapel of St. Ignatius is a Roman Catholic chapel located on Seattle University's campus. Seattle University is a Jesuit Catholic university that was established in Seattle in 1891. Until 25 years ago, however, the university did not have a free-standing chapel. Father Jerry Cobb said, *it was God's providence that held our desire for a chapel in abeyance all those years.* He explained, *when we were finally approved for a chapel, times had changed significantly, and we were able to build a chapel unlike anything we could have built previously.*

St. Ignatius Chapel is a beautiful reward for that patience. In 2022, The American Institute of Architects named the Chapel of St. Ignatius in Seattle, designed by Steven Holl Architects, the winner of its Twenty-Five Year Award, verifying that this design was not only an amazing achievement at the time, but that it is also a design that has stood the test of time.

Father Cobb was chosen by then Seattle University's president to be the client representative on the project, including leading the architect selection team and then participating in the process of designing the new chapel. An architectural competition was held, and the Seattle University team selected Steven Holl Architects to design the chapel. One of the reasons that Father Cobb thought the timing of the new chapel was so perfect is that Seattle had turned into a young, upcoming, high-tech city that was very different from its roots. Catholicism itself was undergoing an update in theology and practice in response to the Second Ecumenical Council of the Vatican of 1965, better known as Vatican II. Seattle University desired a new kind of chapel to present a new kind of church to a new kind of city, and Steven Holl's design tapped into that new spirit beautifully.

Seattle is also one of America's least churched cities, so this new chapel not only needed to speak a new message about the Catholic faith, but it needed to speak it to a new kind of unchurched audience, a condition exacerbated by the fact that it would be on a university campus. According to Father Cobb, they did not want this *to look like your father's church.* The chapel also needed to express the Jesuit tradition of being descriptive rather than prescriptive, consistent with their educational values related to idea exploration. The design team desired, according to Father Cobb, for this chapel to be a *laboratory for discernment.* Father Cobb declared that the *process was as important as the product*, because the process allowed them to truly understand what they most valued, how they wanted to be seen, and how they could communicate those messages through their new chapel.

Steven Holl Architect's design approach adeptly "shape[s] space and light with great contextual sensitivity and to catalyze the unique qualities of each project." The guiding concept for this chapel was *A Gathering of Different Lights*. Per Steven Holl Architect's (Philosophy, n.d.) website, time, space, light, and materials are central, "The phenomena of the space of a room, the sunlight entering through a window, and the color and reflection of materials on a wall and floor all have integral relationships." According to Father Cobb, *the space is designed to create a sense of welcome for people with or without faith and to be experienced as receptive to joy and grief.*

A central question asked during the design process was, *what is sacred space today?* Father Cobb stated that *the ultimate design goal was to produce a sense of the sacred in light.* Holl's design for the chapel is a study in the relationship of new and old, reflecting the new directions of Vatican II in relation to the long history of the Church. It is also a study in how this church can make itself appealing to people without an espoused faith. The design embraces openness, mystery, and humanity.

The chapel design has three main parts, described by Father Cobb as the *field of the not-fully-committed, the reflecting pool, and the chapel*, which represents the hoped-for progression of an unchurched college student. The design of the reflecting pool was inspired by the Zen Garden at Ruōan-ji Temple in Kyoto, Japan, to reflect that it is a place for students (and others) to stop, think, reflect, and contemplate the possibilities of faith and of engaging with the church through the chapel. The raked white gravel pattern of the Ruōan-ji garden, found on the floor of the reflecting pool, is repeated in the plaster pattern of the chapel's interior walls, to continue the motif of reflection. This pool of water also serves to reflect light into the chapel, and its black base is the same color as the black concrete floor of the chapel, creating a continuous reflective surface outside and in.

This idea of reflected light is a very important one for the chapel. One of Holl's (2020) early watercolor sketches for the chapel quoted St. Ignatius himself saying that, "The light to perceive what can be best decided upon must come down from the first and supreme wisdom." Holl (2020) described the chapel as "7 bottles of light in a stone container," signifying there are seven ways and places that light enters the otherwise solid, concrete building. These light bottles allow light to flow in from above, reflect off of colored baffles, and fill the space with various colors of light, which are then reflected again in the black floor. Father Cobb described how the contrast of the light-filled interior with the concrete exterior expresses that *one cannot predict the inside of someone's life from the outside*, and that the light and color within are what really matters. The many curves of the interior create an ambiguous, ever-changing space that Father Cobb described as *interrogative and not declarative*, just as intended. The curves are one

Figure 7.5 Looking across the reflecting pool to the Chapel of St. Ignatius, Seattle, WA. Joe Mabel, CC BY-SA 3.0 <http://creativecommons.org/licenses/by-sa/3.0/>, via Wikimedia Commons.

of the many ways that the chapel expresses humanity and embrace. Details from the altar (that forms the Greek letters Alpha and Omega) to the door handles (that are reminiscent of a priestly stole and are akin to putting one's hands on the shoulders of a friend) express this dynamic, human-centered space as well. Holl even designed a window that reinterprets the traditional Jesuit emblem into one that expresses the brokenness of our current world and Jesus as the answer.

The Chapel of St. Ignatius is a building that is open to the questions of Seattleites and college students, that pulses with the ever-changing light of Seattle, and that expresses ultimately that light overcomes darkness and can bring color into our lives. It has done this extremely well for 25 years and, in so doing, forever changed the perception of Seattle University.

Importance of Architecture and Leadership

In these case studies we find leaders who realize and fully embrace the power of architecture as part of their efforts to communicate values, purpose, and mission; to intentionally inspire and empower those who work inside these buildings as well as those who visit; and to become engaged, contributing citizens and neighbors within their communities.

All five described the importance of the built environment as contextual in terms of natural environment but also of history and community. The DAC design was placed within a city park, a place filled with natural old-growth oak trees and a place of significance to Native American history. A goal of Esri's physical design and siting was that buildings convey a natural sense of emergence from the site. Gensler intentionally diversifies its operations around the world. St, Ignatius desires to reach out to and draw in the surrounding community. Siemens desires to be a good citizen of each place it occupies. We find in these examples buildings deeply rooted within their context; telling a compelling story of their site, people, and mission; perfectly fitted for their time, place, and purpose.

Although those interviewed may have used different language when describing architecture and leadership, all illustrated some aspect of the Critical Components of Architecture, with each employing Building Elements, Design Principles, and Use Strategies to intended effect. The DAC uses circulation, balance, and nature to honor the history of the site, to provide safety for students, and to inspire creativity in the artists who will use the facility. Esri employs scale, balance, site lines, and connections to nature to encourage walking, healthy lifestyles, connections, and mental stimulation for their employees. Gensler's LA office uses scale to announce its size, capacity, and global reach, and circulation, color, and open space to connect to its community and inspire its employees. Siemens uses balance, circulation, and various sensory experiences to create high-tech spaces that convey human interaction and care. St, Ignatius uses light, water, materials, circulation, and proportion to draw students into the mysteries of God.

Upon reflection, when speaking about their organizations, leadership, and architecture, these leaders did not use technical language of form, function, productivity, etc. Instead, leaders told stories about and communicated their emphasis on creating spaces imbued with human values related to contribution, community, creativity, collaboration, communication, and context. Of vital importance to each leader was this idea of creating positive spaces supportive of human flourishing and wellbeing.

We also see in these case studies examples of organizations in which architecture is an integral and strategic part of leadership vision, mission, and purpose in just the ways we have outlined, such as:

- Architecture and leadership dialogically shape an organization's identity, culture, climate, and structure influencing what it will become, reflecting what it has been, and forecasting what it is intended to be.
- Due consideration for organizational (what we value collectively) and individual human values as critical considerations for physical design.

As such, value clarity combined with design intention translate into human and architectural values that can then be incorporated into physical design.

- Learning contributing to flexibility and adaptability of physical design due to shifts in human preferences, needs, and the nature of work, in general.
- The built environment strongly influences and contributes to human flourishing due to attention and intention with regard to Use Strategies: instrumental, physical, social and symbols, esthetics and spiritual, and spatial.
- Affordances contribute to our sense of what is possible within a specific place including the appropriate actions and interactions.
- Architecture can reflect our organizational identity and communicate our organizational stories in powerful ways.
- All leaders, using their own language, distinguished between and considered important: Building Elements, Design Principles, and Use Strategies,

These case studies clearly communicated linkages between and importance of architecture and leadership. Figure 7.6 represents our conceptual understanding of architecture and leadership.

Conclusion

At this point, you've considered architecture and leadership as important; space and place, including how place is filled with meaning and purpose and how architecture defines space; the Critical Components of Architecture: Building Elements, Design Principles, and Use Strategies; and connections between leadership and architecture. Architecture and leadership are value-laden expressions, influencing context, people, and groups, perhaps without our being able to articulate how so. Architecture and leadership contribute to the weaving of the social fabric. Conscientious and purposeful design fosters a sense of agency and action for individuals and groups, contributing to increased contribution, community, creativity, collaboration, and communication. Ultimately, paying attention to the built environment creates a positive experienced space where people feel a sense of community and rootedness to place or context.

Seeing so keenly architecture's influence on people propels us to consider architecture and its role more intently within our organizations. de Botton (2006) described the challenge: "Taking architecture seriously therefore makes some singular and strenuous demands upon us." This is the call to begin with understanding who we are, to create spaces consistent with our

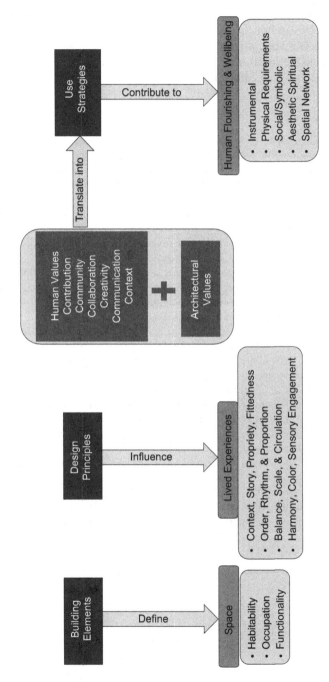

Figure 7.6 Conceptual understanding of architecture. Figure by Mark A. Roberson and Alicia Crumpton.

values, mission, and purpose, and then to select appropriate Building Elements, Design Principles, and Use Strategies to create meaningful places to inhabit. Our hope is that by considering architecture as dialogically informative to the social, we can help leaders create spaces for human flourishing, healing, and community.

References

American Institute of Arts. (2022). *Chapel of St. Ignatius in Seattle Wins AIA's 2022 twenty-five year award*. www.architectmagazine.com/awards/aia-awards/chapel-of-st-ignatius-in-seattle-wins-aias-2022-twenty-five-year-award_o#:~:text=Today%2C%20The%20American%20Institute%20of,2022%20Twenty%2DFive%20Year%20Award

City of Austin, Parks and Recreation Development Dougherty Arts Center (PARD). (2019). Planning and engagement phase. *Presentation to City of Austin Boards and Commission*. www.austintexas.gov/sites/default/files/files/Parks/Dougherty/DAC_Master_Plan/DAC-boards_presentation_20190329.pdf

Cohen, A. (2022). How to make your office an experience multiplier. *Forbes Business Council*. www.forbes.com/sites/forbesbusinesscouncil/2022/05/17/how-to-make-your-office-an-experience-multiplier/?sh=4c67c2f67d39

de Botton, A. (2006). *The architecture of happiness*. Penguin Books.

DLR Group. (n.d.). *Esri campus expansion*. www.dlrgroup.com/work/esri-campus-expansion/

Dougherty Arts Center. (n.d.). *Dougherty arts center*. www.austintexas.gov/department/dougherty-arts-center

Gensler. (n.d.). *About*. www.gensler.com/about

Gensler. (n.d.). *Andy Cohen*. www.gensler.com/people/andy-cohen?l=all

Gensler. (n.d.). *Services*. www.gensler.com/about/services

Gensler Research Institute. (2022). *Design forecast 2022: Resilience*. www.gensler.com/doc/gensler-design-forecast-2022

Holl, S. (2020). *Steven Holl: Inspiration and process in architecture*. Moleskin Books.

Overland Partners. (n.d.). *Culture and practice*. www.overlandpartners.com/culture/

Siemens Healthineers. (n.d.). *Purpose*. www.siemens-healthineers.com/company

Stephen Holl Architects. (n.d.). *Philosophy*. www.stevenholl.com/philosophy/

Index

Note: Page numbers in *italics* indicate a figure and page numbers in **bold** indicate a table on the corresponding page.

Printed in the United States
by Baker & Taylor Publisher Services